FREEDOM FROM THE
INCURABLE ADDICTION
TO SELF

WAITING FOR HEAVEN

LARRY CRABB

First published by Larger Story Press 2020

Copyright © 2020 by Larry Crabb

All rights reserved. No part of this publication may be reproduced, stored or transmitted in any form or by any means, electronic, mechanical, photocopying, recording, scanning, or otherwise without written permission from the publisher. It is illegal to copy this book, post it to a website, or distribute it by any other means without permission. First edition

Paperback ISBN: 978-1-7347350-0-0

Ebook ISBN: 978-1-7347350-1-7

Library of Congress Control Number: 2020907511

Contents

Forward vii
Prologue xi
Introduction xv
A Parable xxi

Part 1: Useful Waiting   1

1: Self-Addiction: An Example 3
2: Was Paul Addicted to Himself? 11
3: One Christian Who Waits. Two Who Don't 15
4: Why Moses? 23
5: Moses Waited! 33
6: Foolish Choices 41

Part 2: Difficult Waiting   51

7: The Struggle for Self-Control 53
8: Is Self-Control Possible? It Depends! 57
9: Passions that Strengthen the Power to Wait 61
10: When the Trinity Came Alive, In Me 67
11: The Power of a Much Needed Vision 75

Part 3: Powerful Waiting   83

12: The Pathway Revealed 85
13: Something More: The Power of Choice 91
14: Wrapping Up: From My Heart to Yours 101
15: All About Me? NO! All About Christ in Me,
    The Hope of Glory 109

Afterword 119
Acknowledgments 123
Notes 125

Forward

BY KEP CRABB

"And I go and prepare a place for you, I will come back and take you to be with me that you also may be where I am" (John 14:3 NIV)[1].

For many years Larry Crabb has been asking hard questions. But the one question my father seems to have wrestled with most has been, "How do people *really* change?" As a clinical psychologist, Dr. Crabb has met with people who were quite literally at the end of life's rope. People who felt they had nowhere to turn as they battled the trials, struggles, pitfalls and addictions that many of us experience and fight today.

What brings people to real change? As a young boy growing up outside Philadelphia, Larry remembers lying in the grassy field behind his Germantown home, gazing up to the clouds and thinking about what heaven will be like. He was aware of something bigger than himself at an early age.

In later years that awareness led him to ask if there really is a heaven, then to ask what will it be like and why don't we think about it more? We think about heaven and take some time to reflect about heaven when a family member or friend dies. And then those thoughts or feelings fade over time and our lives go on. How do we keep heaven in the front position of our minds as we live our lives every day?

Crabb takes the position that if we are aware of the Larger Story God is telling (which has its focus inbetween Christ's Cross and His Coming), then the allure, temptations and distractions of this world won't have the same power over our smaller stories (inbetween our birth and our death). "For this world is not our permanent home; we are looking forward to a home yet to come" (Hebrews 13:14 NLT)[2].

As I worked with Dr. Crabb on this book *Waiting for Heaven,* I found myself keeping heaven more in the forefront of my mind. It slowly began coming up in my awareness as I went through my everyday situations of life. I started to experience some change. I began interacting with my family, friends, and even strangers in a different way. I was feeling a deeper sense of joy as I consciously began to put less importance on this world and my smaller story and pushed heaven and God's Larger Story into a more purposeful spot in my mind. "Friends, this world is not your home, so don't make yourselves cozy in it. Don't indulge your ego at the expense of your soul" (1 Peter 2:11 MSG)[3].

My grandfather used to say that God sometimes gives us a "glimpse of heaven" every now and then to keep us going. It is our hope and prayer that you will experience a "glimpse of heaven" as you read through *Waiting for Heaven: Freedom from the Incurable Addiction to Self.* So, keep your eyes fixed on what is to come, an eternity with Jesus as we worship together in heaven and all things are made new.

"What no eye has seen, nor ear heard, nor the heart of man imagined, what God has prepared for those who love him" (1 Corinthians 2:9 ESV)[4].

Prologue

Christians who refuse to wait for the promised pleasures of heaven remain addicted to their felt well-being, to experiencing consuming satisfaction now. They are fiercely addicted to themselves, and are then powerless to resist whatever temptations promise the sense of well-being they desire.

The result includes addictions to:

drugs, legal or illegal;

food, its compulsive consumption;

sex, both legitimate, illegitimate, and perverted expressions;

money, to the pleasures and convenience and power money can buy;

influence, self-satisfying difference-making pleasure;

recognition, respect that provides personal significance;

and dozens of addictions to other sources of satisfaction that desperate souls crave.

Two Questions

Is there a distinctively Christian way to discover both the will and the ability to rob temptation of its controlling power? Part 1 of this book wrestles with this question and offers direction.

What does victory over the sin of self-centeredness that underlies all addictions look like? Part 2 tackles this question.

Or to put the question another way: what *substantial* victory is available now until *complete* victory comes when we see Jesus? Part 3 outlines a pathway to finding increasing victory now until complete freedom is ours in Heaven.

> "By his divine power, God has given us everything
> we need for living a godly life."
>
> 2 Peter 1:3[1]

Mention the word "addiction" and our minds immediately run to drug, alcohol, and sex addictions. These addictions are very real and far too common. Thankfully, not everyone is plagued by these common struggles. A majority of us (perhaps a slim majority) swallow only physician prescribed drugs, enjoy only an occasional glass of wine or a couple beers while watching a game on television, and live only within moral boundaries of sexual activity. And that's good.

Here's the bad news. Another addiction exists, a rarely recognized one operating covertly to at least some degree in virtually every human being but one since Adam and Eve. Throughout post-Eden history, each one of us has arrived in this world with a stubborn commitment to our own felt well-being. We then live addicted to arranging for satisfaction of whatever longings we can neither deny nor smother.

To understand and recognize how this addiction plays itself out, we need to remember that we are relational beings, created in the image of the three-person relational God. It's natural then, and not wrong, to look for the satisfaction we cannot provide for ourselves through relationships. But there is a problem. We've moved away from looking to God for the satisfaction our relational souls crave which then frees us to focus on finding satisfaction in other relationships that God makes possible.

Because we have moved away from God for our core satisfaction, we now expect and even feel entitled to core satisfaction from relationships with others. But things don't go so well. Two bankrupt people wanting money from the other leaves both of them broke.

As a consequence, we have learned to:
- **protect** ourselves from hurt by others;
- **procure** from others what enhances our favored image of ourselves;
- **preserve** that image by letting others see only what maintains it.

The result? **Relational Sin,** a failure to love others the way Jesus loved us. It's the universal human addiction, an epidemic: relating in the self-focused energy of self-protection designed to not hurt; self-procurement angling to enhance through others our easily threatened self-esteem; and self-preservation shielding our self-image from further injury. Relational sin plants the seeds of the quarrels, fights, and jealousies that James warns us about (see James 4:1-3)[2]. Relational poverty then develops in families, communities, churches, nations and the world.

Now the point: my central purpose in writing this book is to encourage movement away from relational sin to relational holiness, an embraced and lived commitment to delighting God by how we relate to Him and to others, worshipping God and building up others.

Waiting till heaven for the complete satisfaction of our relational longings (then we actually will fully love God and others) will supply strength to better combat addictions to drugs, alcohol and sex. If, however, we replace relational poverty with relational wealth by overcoming to an always developing degree our universal addiction to self, our incurable relational addiction will find its corrective in waiting for heaven to provide what is not fully available now. We'll then love better, more like Jesus, and in the process discover joy.

Interested? Read on!

Introduction

In 1988, I published a book titled *Inside Out*. The opening paragraph read as follows:

"Modern Christianity, in dramatic reversal of its biblical form, promises to relieve the pain of living in a fallen world. The message, whether it's from fundamentalists requiring us to live by a favored set of rules or from charismatics urging a deeper surrender to the Spirit's power, is too often the same: the promise of bliss is for NOW! Complete satisfaction can be ours this side of heaven."[1]

If I were editing that paragraph today, I wouldn't change a word. But I might add a couple. I would consider adding this closing sentence: "*There is no need to wait for the satisfaction of your deepest desire; it's available in this life.*" That sentence would only provide assurance that further compounds the egregious error that marked Christianity as the 20th century came to an end.

I fear that what I recognized then is still in evidence today. Too much of what passes for Christianity in our current evangelical culture remains revised from its biblical form but has now sunk even deeper into the quicksand of appealing teaching that wrongly suggests what it means to follow Jesus.

Therefore, I want to begin this book with an updated paragraph that highlights what appears to be a more pressing concern today. This paragraph is a little longer than the former one, reflecting that we may now be even more off track than before.

> *Modern Christianity, in its misguided focus on using God to make this life work well for us, has lost the passion of eagerly waiting for Jesus to return to make all things new. Why wait for then when with God's favor we can arrange now for this life to work pretty well? We can make those prayer-supported arrangements while Jesus remains at the Father's right-hand directing God's Spirit to see to it that life's circumstances bring happiness to His followers.*

> *As a result, we can bypass any ongoing need for lament. The consistently upbeat words and hand-clapping tunes sung Sunday mornings in many churches lead people into excited worship. A dangerously wrong idea is thus deeply but subtly ingrained in today's Christianity: the ability to love well and the power to experience joy depend on favorable circumstances, circumstances promised by God that make up the good life. The Spirit's role to form Christ in us is thereby minimized if not eliminated. Has modern Christianity accommodated itself to our prevailing addiction to ourselves while deceiving us into believing we are enlightened and mature?*

Well, one paragraph grew into two. I think both were needed to hear the message that is shouted from many pulpits and enticingly written about in many books: No longer must we wait for the next life to know the joy and freedom we long to experience. Since what we most want is fully available now, no longer must we work hard to stay faithful to God and useful to others. Both come easily in our pleasant God-blessed lives.

Our culture has opted for Casual Christianity, a religion that, among other essential disciplines, has given up rigorously discerning self-examination that reveals what is ugly in us and what is our impact on others. When practiced, that discipline leads us toward the joy of repentance that moves us away from self-centered relating into humble other-centeredness. We live too often with our felt well-being as our priority concern, incurably addicted to ourselves. And because we think Jesus shares that priority, we believe we're living the Christian life. Casual Christianity has become Counterfeit Christianity, a different gospel which Paul strongly warned us against (see Galatians 1:6).[2]

The consequences of such thinking are many, each one damaging to the cause of Christ. One consequence – and I believe it is central – is this: *The absence of waiting for complete satisfaction till heaven begets the presence of addiction, a demand to feel pain-numbing delight in this life.* There is no question that addictions soil our souls, adding power to our natural self-centeredness which, because it feels necessary for our felt well-being, is accepted as justified, not terribly sinful. We insist on experiencing an intensity of consuming pleasure that quiets all worry and fear if only for a few moments. We then live a life style of arranging for successive short-lived experiences that achieve our goal of nirvana, a Buddha-like sense of heavenly peace. As a result, addictions, growing out of our core universal addiction to our selves, eventually take control of our lives. The energy and motivation needed to serve the cause of Christ gets badly short-changed.

That's the bad news. Here's the good news. Biblical Christianity provides a way to rise up from this quicksand: *Waiting!* But waiting for heaven to provide what our hearts most long to experience is no longer in vogue. And yet learning to eagerly wait for the Lord's return is essential to overcoming the root demand beneath all addictions. But even as I write those words, words I believe to be true, I sense within me an uncomfortable hesitation: *the choice to wait is easy to state but hard to make.* The longing within us for more urgently presses for satisfaction. And there are ways to arrange for an experience, though temporary and counterfeit, that quiets the demands of our thirsty souls.

Waiting becomes even more difficult and seemingly an unreasonable path to follow when we feel saddened by loss or discouraged over setbacks or resentful when mistreated or just weary with life. It is then the temptation is strongest to arrange for moments of anesthetizing pleasure. Sin warmly invites us to enjoy its delights.

I am writing this book to explore what it will take to so absorbingly anticipate the satisfaction fully available in heaven that no difficulty now will have the power to render any relief-promising temptation irresistible. I've neither read in Christian books or studied in Christian psychology or pondered in Christian categories of thought an answer to that question that works for me. But, a quick caveat: I believe there is no path to walk that eliminates the struggle to resist temptation or that guarantees no further failure. Our addiction is incurable until Heaven, but we could be moving into greater freedom from it as we live in this world.

I believe that there is a biblically derived, Spirit-guided, Christ-dependant, Father-honoring way to overcome addictions to the degree that we can meaningfully be with others pouring supernatural life out of us into them. The prospect of discovering that way excites me, and transforms book writing into a spiritual adventure. The verse I earlier quoted adds to the excitement. "By his divine power, God has given us everything we need for living a godly life" (2 Peter 1:3)[3]. A godly life will not be under the control of addictions.

A Parable

There was a man, a good decent Christian man. Like every other man, Christian or not, this man thirsted for respect. Private questions plagued him. Am I worth notice? Do I matter? He longed to be known, known and respected. And wanted. His thirst was real, and deep.

But he was afraid to be fully known. Were he to be seen all the way through by another, he was convinced he would experience well deserved shame in the presence of another's disgust.

And yet he yearned for the impossible, to be fully known by someone who would draw near to him and never back away. But why dream the impossible dream? Better to hide from others behind a false front, an appearance of strength, confidence; perhaps compassion and concern for others. Better to live for whatever satisfaction he could arrange for himself, sometimes from others. Anything to relieve the emptiness of unquenched thirst, an intolerable ache.

If all else failed to provide the desired relief, porn reliably worked. Was he sexually addicted? The possibility assaulted his conscience. But he could mute the sense of conviction. Relief from thirst seemed necessary, and therefore justified. Living in the emptiness and exhaustion of unsatisfied desire could not be endured.

There was a woman, a kind competent Christian woman. Like every other woman, Christian or not, this woman thirsted for notice. Private questions plagued her. Could I be seen and still desired? Do I have value for who I am? She longed to be noticed, no longer invisible, and appreciated. Her thirst was real, and deep.

But she was afraid to be fully seen. Would another's discerning glance into her depths reveal a beauty in her being, in her soul; a beauty that mattered, that would be desired by another who longed for rich relationship and for partnership in an important purpose? Were she to be fully visible to another, would she feel self-contempt in the presence of another's movement away from her?

And yet she couldn't stop wanting the impossible, to be fully seen by another who would draw near to her with respect and appreciation for who she was. But to risk dreaming the impossible dream risked feeling the emptiness of aloneness. Better to hide from others behind a false front; friendly sociability and charm, perhaps achievement in a profession coupled with the appearance of sure-footedness. Anything to numb the painful void of unsatisfied longing, the seething simmering of unquenched thirst.

If she couldn't quiet her unrelieved thirst beneath the satisfaction of lesser thirsts, perhaps an intentional display of sexuality could provide a convincing semblance of true satisfaction. But would she stoop to cheapening herself that way? It would nearly destroy whatever was left of her self esteem. Perhaps she had no other option. Living in the emptiness of an agonizing ache and with the exhaustion of unsatisfied thirst could not be endured.

Out of nowhere, both the man and woman heard a voice, it seemed a Voice from heaven.

> "You may continue to fight against the ache in your heart and the thirst in your soul, experiencing them both as unendurable; and you will then embrace and yield to temptation that numbs your ache and relieves your thirst. But I want you to know this: I will never love you less.
>
> "You will, however, fail to grasp the freedom of resting in my love. Continue on the road you are now traveling that delivers only the illusion of life, and your soul will shrink. Your capacity, your passion, and your resolve to love will diminish, corrupted by the evil of self-centeredness that curves you away from others and toward your self.
>
> "To become the person you're most thirsty to be; to live as a teller of the Larger Story I scripted in eternity past and am now unwrapping in this present fallen world; to expand your capacity to love others more than yourself; and to anchor your hope in the anticipated joy of what lies ahead when your ache will completely disappear and when your thirst will be forever fully satisfied, you must be willing now to live thirsty.
>
> "Only then will you experience the ruling desire and know the sufficient power to fight your addiction to claiming now what I promise only for later, forgotten ache and

satisfied thirst. Yielding to addictive urges does no more than mask your ache and narcotisize your thirst.

"The struggle is real. Resisting addictive urges will not be easy. You will fail. But joy, the joy of loving grace is on the horizon. The sun is rising".

The man heard the Voice, hung his head in shame as he resigned himself to inevitable failure, then turned a deaf ear to what he had heard. He regarded the ache in his heart as a disorder, suffering that Christianity should eliminate. And he continued to fight against the thirst in his soul as an enemy of joy. Whatever was required to satisfy that thirst seemed somehow legitimate, a necessity to living without an aching heart and an unquenched thirst. He refused to LIVE THIRSTY. It made no sense.

The woman heard the same Voice, hung her head in brokenness and repentance, then with a taste of freedom and surrendered to the hope stirred by the Voice, and with eyes wide open entered the battle to embrace both the ongoing ache in her heart and the exhaustion of unquenched thirst, no longer assuming she was entitled to a life on earth with neither a throbbing ache nor an unsatisfied desire. She engaged the struggle to fight against and resist sinful opportunities to numb her ache and relieve her thirst. She responded to the call to LIVE THIRSTY. It made perfect sense.

Joy was available as she tasted God to be present in her darkness. And peace, peace that, without eliminating her ache or weakening her thirst, could anchor her soul in hope and become an experienced truth that would soon bring her rest in life's storms. She could then envision addiction to relief losing its power as she waited for the eternal day of perfect rest.

> ***"If only for this life we have hope in Christ,***
> ***we are to be pitied more than all men."***
> *I Corinthians 15:19[1]*

BUT
If our hope in Christ is firmly anchored
in the next life,
then we of all people can be most satisfied now.
therefore
LIVE THIRSTY!

And Wait, for what only Heaven offers.

Our addiction to ourselves brings on the loneliness of relational poverty. But dependence on what Christ provides now as we wait for all that lies ahead keeps us persevering on the narrow road with grateful anticipation.

PART I

USEFUL WAITING

It's Value

CHAPTER ONE

Self-Addiction: An Example

I just noticed a clear example of a cowardly tendency of mine. This example managed to turn on the proverbial light, brightly. With disturbing clarity I'm seeing that a self-protective fainthearted tendency within me reflects to a frightening degree that feeling good means more to me than loving well, at least sometimes. This is one of those times.

It's early Sunday morning. I've spent the last several hours reading a little book titled *"How to Die"*, a compilation of an ancient sage's thoughts on the matter. Seneca, a first century Roman philosopher, an early Stoic, lost favor with Nero after serving more than a decade as his mentor and advisor. In a fit of irrational anger, the deranged emperor ordered his faithful companion to kill himself. Seneca willingly obeyed and brought on his own death, in 65 A.D. In the years before his suicide, the respected philosopher had written extensively to friends and followers proposing what it would mean to die a good death after living a good life. It's quite likely Seneca thought he scored well on both counts.

James S. Romm, a professor of classics at Bard College, translated and edited Seneca's voluminous writings and published *"How to Die"* in 2018. When I happened across the title, I bought the book and eagerly opened it. I'm no longer young. I thought the ancient philosopher might have something interesting to say, perhaps something personally helpful.

But a shameful tendency became more visible to me as I slowly read the 121 pages of Romm's English translation. Another 90 pages record Seneca's material in its original Latin which, despite two years of high school Latin, I couldn't read, not a word.

True to his stoicism, Seneca was telling me how I could face death without fear if I lived a good life from which one day I could nobly exit. Few if any of his recommendations struck me as worth considering. My strong disagreement with his teaching, to which I'm entitled, developed into a cavalier smugness toward Seneca, to which I'm not entitled.

Three examples will make the point. In each one I briefly quote Seneca then record what in reaction went through my mind.

Example #1:

Seneca: "He lives badly who does not know how to die well." (p.4.)[1]

Me: "Where does this guy get off pontificating on such a weighty topic? If he seriously wanted to know how to live a purposeful life then die a purposeful death, realizing that a good life and death are both purposeful, he could have studied the life and death of Jesus. Three of the four gospel records of Christ's life and death, Matthew, Mark, and Luke, were written before Seneca died. Seneca became a young senator in Rome a few years after Jesus was crucified. It's likely he at least heard of Jesus. And yet he doesn't give a second look into the wisest man who ever lived. And I'm supposed to revere Seneca's good judgment?"

Example #2:
Seneca: "Make your life joyful by putting aside all anxiety about keeping it" (p. 104)[1].
Me: "Easier said then done. Is Seneca telling me to live in denial of the possibility of a painful death in order to not mind dying? Or is he suggesting that the desire to stay alive is somehow unhealthy? Only Christianity makes it possible to face death, even a painful death, with comfort-disturbing yet gladly anticipated joy, not the prospect of painless non-existence (if there is such a thing), but the joy of knowing that every self-aware Christian wants most what lies ahead on the other side of death. Like a good Stoic, Seneca values undisturbed peace, Buddha-like peace, as a person's greatest good. But Christianity offers a Jesus-like peace that *supports* us in living and loving well even when life is disappointing and heartbreaking. Jesus-like peace doesn't *suffocate* the pain, it *releases* purpose through pain. Is there no place for peace-disturbing lament in Seneca's formula for a good life and death? It would seem he wants us to whistle a pleasant tune as we stroll through a cemetery."

Example #3:
Seneca: "… what news is it that someone has died whose life was nothing else than a journey toward death?" (p. 98)[1].
Me: "Seneca is wrong, yet again. For a Christian, existence is a journey through a God-delighting life, a meaningful and joyful if imperfect and difficult journey that is moving on a straight path to the never ending joy everyone longs to fully experience. This supposedly brilliant philosopher is missing out on the foundational truth that makes life good and makes death far better, forever. No doubt Seneca's intelligence quotient would rank him in the genius category, but the man was a fool."

I don't suppose you missed the odor of uncharitable smugness leaking out of me toward this lost fool, an attitude devoid of even the faintest fragrance of love. As I read his writings, I felt not even a dash of burdened concern for Seneca's soul. I affirm the Christian perspectives I stated but I'm shamed by the merciless passion with which I expressed them.

But why? Why the self-stained attitude? Why the ego building pleasure in asserting what I know that Seneca didn't? What was going on in me that poured out in such a sub-Christian manner toward a fellow human being whom God loves? A few undeveloped thoughts:

- Is my felt superiority a defensive maneuver? Does it defend me against some hidden threat?
- Could my arrogant dogmatism be protecting me from a profound spiritual discomfort I don't want to face?
- Am I scared? Is there a dread lodged deep within me – a dread of some extremely disquieting terror – that when touched provokes more than a hint of anger? Might my anger perversely stir up the good feelings I crave?

An uncomfortable thought: if I were the truly convinced and committed Christian I sometimes believe I am, a man settled firmly in longing to live for Jesus at any cost as I wait patiently for the no-cost already-paid-for life that awaits me when I die, would I react to stubbornly wrong teaching with such snobby smugness? Might I be a Christian poseur, little more than a spiritual persona impressing others with apparent maturity while I look down my nose on those who hold to a foolish misunderstanding about life? Wouldn't a mature disciple, a resolute imitator of Christ, feel a compassionate burden for the countless Senecas who have life figured out all wrong?

I have little choice but to draw a regrettable conclusion: something is seriously off track in my faith. I think I now know what it is. No doubt much else is off track, and I anticipate the Spirit's light shining even more brightly in the days ahead on my twisted faith. No one gets everything right this side of heaven. But there is one significant lack that is now visible to my partially Spirit-enlightened mind. And I'm grateful that I'm seeing it. It augurs well; more growth is on its way. What I am now recognizing in me, deficient faith in a particular form, seems important enough, troubling enough, and common enough to write about it. Hence, this book.

I'm surprised. Since the publication of my most recent book, *When God's Ways Make No Sense*[2], I've been wondering, with not a little bit of relief, if maybe I don't have another book in me, one I firmly want to write. Maybe I've written all the books God had in mind to bear my name on the front cover. Maybe it's time to wrap up my writing career. Age, the arbiter of much that we do and don't do, may be speaking to me.

And then this: a hard-to-resist urge to do some concerted thinking about a flaw in my understanding of life that I doubt is unique to me. Perhaps it is dangerously widespread and widely unrecognized in Christian community. If not seen and confessed in a way that leads to conviction, repentance, and freedom, this lack, this misunderstanding of the spiritual journey, could be keeping many of us skipping about in ankle-deep Christianity thinking we've bravely dived into the deep end of the pool.

What am I discerning that the Spirit's revealing light is exposing in the realms of darkness still within me? It's this:

A REFUSAL TO WAIT!

I want now, in this life, what God only promises for later, in the next life. I'm aware that when Jesus returns He will make all things new. But couldn't He straighten out a few more things before then?

There are times I get impatient with God. I don't always appreciate the plot He has come up with for how my life is unfolding.

Among much else, I want an experience in this life that shuts out all the stress brought on by difficulties, that numbs all my insecurity, that pleasantly weakens my awareness of failure. I want such an experience, if even for only a few delicious moments. But God disappoints me. He seems only to give me what supports my walk with Jesus even as difficulties mount, insecurity deepens, and egregious failures continue. I am convinced I need something else.

I'm never free of concern that more trouble is waiting around the next bend. I never rest so completely in God's boundless love that all remnants of insecurity disappear. And I never become so compelled by God's good plan for my life that sin loses all appeal. The result? I sometimes take matters into my own hands to provide for myself the experience I want, a kind of pleasure so consuming that trouble seems far away, that rejection no longer scares me, and that failure becomes either unrecognized or unconvicting.

If Peter were speaking to me right now, I think I know a little of what he would say. In his old age, not too long before he was crucified upside down, he wrote a letter to several groups of Christians whose lives were not going well. They were suffering. *And Peter told them to not let relief become their goal.* Instead he warmly encouraged these hard pressed believers in God's goodness to put their "hope fully on the grace that will be brought" to them, not in this life, but "at the revelation of Jesus Christ," (I Peter 1:13)[3], referring to His second coming when He will make all things new, right every wrong, dry every tear, and satisfy every longing alive in our glorified souls.

Until then Peter tells us, *Wait!* What we most want lies ahead. Demand nothing now. Expect everything then. Receive every good thing that comes to you now. Enjoy each one, with thanks. But realize this life will never fully satisfy your deepest thirst. Paul agrees with Peter. He told the Roman Christians to continue to "groan inwardly" and to "wait eagerly" (Romans 8:23)[4].

A Christian who is waiting to later receive everything the human heart longs for while reason for lament continues now will not satisfy his or her ego as I did and sometimes still do, by responding to someone's wrong thinking, whether in Seneca or a spouse or child or friend, with patronizing smugness that elevates one's self above another, an elevation that feels, can I say it? – damn good, a feeling that smells of pride and is therefore worthy of damning. Is this nuanced proof of my hidden relational addictions?

Waiting on God's timetable, frustrating though it may be, will free us to live a good life now marked by increasingly consistent self-denying other-centeredness and always deepening appreciation of forgiveness, no longer so caught up in providing for our own good feelings, for ecstatic but shallow temporary pleasure.

Waiting Christians will more quickly recognize temptation for what it is, an opportunity to arrange for oneself an experience that God promises to provide later. And waiting Christians will discover new strength to resist the allure of such opportunities. Christians who learn to wait will live a better life now and will die a better death when heaven's gates swing open. Could this be the narrow road to freedom?

Lord, teach me to wait.

> *"Jesus, here I am again,*
> *desiring a thing that were I to indulge in it*
> *would war against my heart and the hearts*
> *of those I love.*
> *In this moment I might choose to indulge a*
> *fleeting hunger or I might choose to love you more.*

Given the choice of shame or glory,
let me choose glory.
Given the choice of this moment or eternity,
let me choose in this moment what is eternal.
Given the choice of this easy pleasure,
or the harder road of the cross,
Give me grace to choose to follow you".[5]

WAIT

CHAPTER TWO

Was Paul Addicted to Himself?

For many years, I've taken somewhat perverse comfort in Paul's description of his Christian experience in Romans 7. With remarkable candor, in that chapter the man we rightly know as the great apostle Paul confirmed that "all kinds of covetous desires" were within him (verse 8)[1]. I wonder what they were. Would they match mine?

With that recognition, he had little choice but to realize that something was terribly wrong. He openly admitted that "the trouble is with me, for I am all too human, a slave to sin" (verse 14)[1]. And yet at the beginning of his letter to the Christians in Rome he introduced himself as "a slave to Christ Jesus, chosen by God to be an apostle and sent out to preach his Good News" (Romans 1:1)[2]. Was Martin Luther right? Are we all both sinners and saints?

Or was Paul a special case, a living contradiction, both a slave to sin and a slave of Christ Jesus? The comfort I draw from Paul centers in my understanding that he is telling me, as does Luther, that even a genuinely devoted follower of Jesus still struggles mightily with sin, and sometimes fails. Such comfort becomes perverse, however, when it lets me feel complacent about my failure. Perhaps one difference in a deeply committed disciple of Christ and a more casual Jesus follower is that the former is more aware of his or her ongoing struggle with sin, and hates each failure. But assuming that our battle against sin becomes more intense not less intense as we mature, how exactly is that good news?

What am I to learn from Paul when in Romans 7 he goes on to say, "I don't really understand myself."? Nor do I. And then he adds, "I want to do what is right, but I don't do it. Instead I do what I hate"[3]. So do I. You'll find those words in verse 15. Those severe recognitions were owned by a man who many have understandably referred to as the greatest Christian who ever lived.

To make sure we don't casually move past what Paul is telling us, he tells us once more, "I don't want to do what is wrong, but I do it anyway" (verse 19)[3]. Me too. Remember my snippy jabs at Seneca. Ugly proud snippiness flowed outward from deep places within me, places not yet purified. Cheeky words came out of me as spontaneously as a sneeze when I have a cold.

I am now seeing myself as a diagnosable addict. Somewhere in his writings Luther not only declared that every Christian is both sinner and saint but also that we are all addicts – to self. I long for relief from the sadness and struggle of living as a still fallen man with fallen people in a fallen world. Jesus promised that one day He would return and do away with every remnant of fallenness. But life is painful and so I too easily refuse to wait. I do whatever it takes to find the relief I crave, and to feel it now.

I've learned my strategies, effective ones, for feeling good. I know how to quickly and reliably stir up wonderfully pleasant, even fulfilling emotions that come with an intensity that seems to drown whatever feelings I find disturbing. For a few delicious moments, I'm at peace with myself and with life. Or so it seems. I don't easily recognize that this kind of peace weakens my ability and my desire to love. I'm feeling too good to worry about someone else and whether I'm loving them well.

Was that Paul's experience? Did he sometimes do whatever it takes to feel good? I don't know. Even he had an abundance of soul disappointments and relational difficulties on his journey to heaven. Did Paul hate his sinful lapses while delighting in the relief, the numbing pleasure they brought? Hebrews warns us against the "fleeting pleasures of sin" (Hebrews 11:25)[4]. But they work, for those few delicious moments. Do any of us resolutely heed that warning, with unwavering steadfastness?

We may be registered guests on the ship sailing to heaven. But when strong winds raise high waves in the water, do we change course? Do we push aside the ship's experienced and confident captain and grab the wheel, turning it in hopes of finding smoother sailing? Or do we wait, trusting Captain Jesus to bring us through choppy waters to a safe harbor? If not, why? A question worth asking.

CHAPTER THREE

One Christian Who Waits. Two Who Don't

It's one thing to talk about an idea. It's quite another to know someone who lives, or doesn't live, what you're talking about. As I write this book, I'm visualizing three folks I know, each a professing sincere follower of Jesus. One waits for the joys of heaven, demanding nothing now, patiently enduring every hardship, disappointment, and failure. Another hears the call from God to wait, recognizes its intended value and speaks warmly about anticipating heaven's glories, but finds neither joy nor transforming power in waiting and therefore doesn't. Still another sees no need to wait for the satisfaction promised in heaven. Life now is quite satisfying. Later pleasures are appreciated as a mildly welcome add on, the proverbial cherry on a sundae.

These three Christians illustrate three categories of men and women each of whom sincerely claim to be following Jesus.

Category #1: Committed Christians

In this group, unfortunately a small minority, the believers know Jesus well enough to want, more than anything else, to be with Him, in measure now, beyond measure later. The mere anticipation of actually seeing Jesus in person brings them more joy than any pleasure available in this world. They long to experience now, and often do, a taste of the banquet they will forever enjoy in the coming world where there is no sorrow, struggle or sin. These Christians realize that the richest satisfaction this world can provide doesn't match the taste of God's goodness now, and without question falls infinitely short of heaven's eternal joys.

Those tastes further intensify their longing to savor the entire meal, and in the process put them more in touch with their desires for a depth of satisfaction that will never be experienced until either they die or Jesus returns. Much to their regret, that unquenched thirst tempts them, if even for a brief moment, to somehow arrange for a more meaningful experience of fullness in their souls. The temptation might be as seemingly innocent as saying something to someone that displays their wisdom and insight, or doing something for someone in order to evoke praise for their kindness and charity.

The temptation is real. But most often (not always), when it rises up with relentless appeal, these Christians intentionally recall three truths: what Jesus did for them through His death; that the Spirit of Christ, embodying Christ's divine nature as a human, is alive within them; and that Jesus endured inexpressible agony without arranging for relief, longing for the joy that would follow, and in the process providing an example to follow: first suffering then glory.

And then a quiet but compelling desire is reliably aroused in these thirsty believers, but now not only a longing to feel fullness of soul in this life but an even stronger wish to delight God by neither saying or doing what they clearly discern would be self-serving. And they celebrate the truth that delighting God brings unmatched delight to their souls. A vision comes into focus, a vision of being an ingredient in the divine happiness (as C.S. Lewis once put it)[1], a vision of becoming someone whose way of life inspires others to walk the same path.

This category of person both hears and heeds the call to wait, to demand no satisfaction that this world can provide while gratefully enjoying every God-designed blessing that comes their way; to hate the illusion of satisfaction that sin generates; and to wait in certain hope and in enlivening anticipation of heaven's joys. This freedom from self ushers in freedom in other areas of temptation and addiction.

To all in this category, I say: *Keep on!* You're on the narrow road to the life you most desire both now and then. And to myself I say: *Be smart, do whatever it takes to be found among these waiting Christians.*

Category #2: Casual Christians

Too many Christians fit into this second category, most (hopefully) longing to belong to Category #1. They battle against a favorite passion, a strong temptation to indulge a certain yearning that when indulged reliably creates deep in their soul a unique pleasure, a satisfaction that they experience as both strangely foreign yet wonderfully freeing and intimate, but intimate with only themselves. This delightful experience stirs a pleasure that nothing else can stir so well. Neither loving someone meaningfully or praying fervently or worshipping God passionately with hands held high can offer this remarkably delicious, worry-numbing experience brought on by yielding to this temptation. The sensation somehow feels complete, blocking out pressing fears, unpleasant thoughts, and disturbing emotions that too often unsettle these Casual Christians. No other legitimate pleasure, no tasty meal, no grand vacation, no high spirits felt when they buy their dream house or a new car can so effectively and reliably do the same.

These people are Christians. Like Committed Christians, when their choice temptation assails them, they often, and sometimes desperately, bring Christ's death to mind and feel sincere gratitude for the grace of forgiveness. They genuinely believe that Christ's Spirit is alive in them, but they feel little of His presence. But they do sense an inner stirring to please the Father by resisting the temptation. And thoughts of heaven may come to mind, but rarely, if ever, with gripping force. Avoiding pain and enjoying pleasure have become more compelling.

Yet the felt gratitude for what Jesus has done, the awareness that the Spirit is nudging them in a good direction, and the anticipated joys of Christ's coming, together cannot measure up to the settled illusion of peaceful wholeness they feel when the temptation is indulged. For seasons, some as short as a few days, some as long as months, these believers manage to say no to the tempting pleasures. Then it happens again. They give in, and another season of seemingly irresistible failure begins. During these seasons, they fail, not always but often.

Casual Christians try to "white knuckle" it, waiting for the incomparable delights promised in heaven and denying themselves the enjoyment of unclean pleasures now. But they inevitably find themselves arranging for the predictably reliable satisfaction available on demand. They are frustrated with themselves – "why do I lack self control?; with life – "life always throws me a curve. Pressure mounts and relief seems necessary."; and with God – "shouldn't He be doing more to help me?". Indulging their loved yet hated temptation leaves them with a sense of uneasy guilt that fades into indifference and angry resignation. They focus on the presenting addiction instead of the underlying self-addiction and miss the true nature of the battle.

To the scores of Jesus followers in this category, I say: *Don't quit! Don't leave the battle ground.* Defeat is *not* inevitable. There is more to the Gospel than you now know, more that can surface the liberated will already within you, the will to wait and obey. You will discover the thirst in your soul, the sincere desire to wait for the authentic version of the counterfeit pleasure, the false pleasure that is warring against your soul even as you experience it. And to myself, I say: Trust your thirst to delight God and wait for Jesus: *to whatever degree you fit into Category #2, realize that you long to be elsewhere.*

Category #3: Complacent Christians

This is the most dangerous of the three categories. Those who belong in this category have convinced themselves that they truly are committed to Christ, living comfortably committed to Christianity as they understand it. They remain unaware that they live in self-protection and for self-enhancement: "I want to feel safe and I want to feel good". Their wish is granted, and they praise God for His faithfulness in providing the blessings that grant their wish. Life is working: a relatively happy marriage with wonderful kids, or a happily contented life as a single, good health, and enough money to live well.

Many in this category have a ministry that offers the opportunity to display their talents and resources. A good number of them often attend conferences, listening to notable Christian leaders whose teaching they affirm and believe they are following. Some are pastors.

When worship music in church or a conference directs their thoughts to the Lord's love so fully revealed at Calvary and to His soon coming, these Christians experience what they think is joy but without recognizing the smug attitude beneath their pleasant emotions. In their minds, rarely acknowledged, a belief is strengthened: Jesus died not only to forgive their sins but also to now show favor to His forgiven followers by blessing them with whatever they need to enjoy life. And blessings that bring a comfortable life are valued above the blessing that brings forgiveness and the ability to love others at great cost to themselves. The divine voice that calls them to wait, and as they wait to place priority on spiritual growth and on spiritually blessing others, is drowned out by a louder voice that assures them they are entitled to life's blessings, blessings that free them to live the good life. This understanding of the pattern of God's blessings is more evidence of a deceptive and entrenched addiction to self.

To complacent professing Christians, I say: *Wake up!* You are living in Laodicea, if not downtown at least in its suburbs. Consider Paul's words to the Corinthians, "Examine yourselves to see if your faith is genuine" (2 Corinthians 13:5)[2]. In another place he wrote: "… on the judgment day, fire will reveal what kind of work each builder has done. The fire will show if a person's work has any value… But if the work is burned up, the builder will suffer great loss. The builder will be saved, but like someone barely escaping through a wall of flames" (1 Corinthians 3:13-15)[3].

You are too deeply asleep to hear the Spirit's call to wait. You must first hear Him warn you of the coming day of judgment for all Christians. On that day you may hear Jesus say, "Not well done". Today your anticipation of His coming is weak. Your hope is fixed on a pleasantly blessed life now rather than on a gloriously blessed life then that could free you in this life to live to delight the Father by yielding to the Spirit's work of forming you like Jesus. To myself I say: *God forbid that I am a Complacent Christian.*

I suspect close examination will reveal that most of us can be identified as belonging to one of these three categories, or perhaps wobbling through all three. It might do us good to take a careful look at one God-follower who learned to wait, who provides a striking example of a Category #1 believer, a Committed Christian, someone who waited.

The Bible tells the story of an Old Testament man who gave up a much-blessed life to follow God on the path of a much-troubled life. Moses heard the call to wait for a greater reward than this life can offer, no matter how blessed, a reward so great that in comparison "present troubles are small" (2 Corinthians 4:17)[4]. We'll look at the life of Moses. Perhaps the Spirit will use his journey to illumine the path to becoming a Category #1 Christian, a Jesus follower who actively waits for Jesus to return.

CHAPTER FOUR

Why Moses?

Consider a familiar biblical passage where its author Paul was evidently writing his words with an impelling sense of both excitement and privilege. First, he tells us that God "is so rich in kindness and grace that he purchased our freedom with the blood of his Son and forgave our sins". Paul then seems especially moved as he goes on to say that God "has now revealed to us his mysterious will regarding Christ – which is to fulfill his own good plan" (Ephesians 1:7-9 NLT)[1].

And we Christians, living in a broken world as broken people, with great interest ask, what exactly is God's plan, and what makes it good when too much badness surrounds us and when so much badness within us competes with whatever goodness has been planted in us by God's Spirit?

In verse 10, Paul quickly replies "… this is the plan"[2], then spends ten more verses giving us a clear look into the Larger Story of God, a story that provides solid reason to wait for its completion and to live well now. Listen to verse 14 with a few additional clarifying comments of my own:

"The Spirit is God's guarantee" for now "that he will give us the inheritance he promised", so therefore wait in confident anticipation of what's coming; "and that he has purchased us to be his own people"; we're to live now as God's chosen people. And here's the entire point of the plan: "He did this so we would praise and glorify him"[2].

Another question immediately comes to our minds: "what does it mean to glorify God"? Paul told the Corinthians that he was sending Titus and "another brother" to their church and that this other brother would accompany Paul as he took the money donated by the Corinthian believers to Jerusalem, "a service that glorifies the Lord and shows our eagerness to help" (2 Corinthians 8:19 NLT)[3].

I suggest that for us to glorify the Lord in this corrupted world, among other activities and attitudes, means to reveal God's uncorrupted disposition to love others by how we relate to them, being with others with a genuine longing to encourage them. It's clear that what we might call *divine outwardness* lies in the center of God's dynamic being. It is a passionate disposition made obvious in His willingness to do whatever was needed by Him to pour His love into us so that in always increasing measure we might pour that love into others. In so doing we glorify God, by revealing His essence to those around us. And we glorify God by living in the confidence and pleasure of knowing that His love is never one whit compromised by the struggles and sorrow and sin that we experience while we wait for the climax, the eternal consummation of the Larger Story.

Yet another question rises up: is it possible to live like that? Of course God knew we would ask that question. Throughout the Bible He therefore recorded the stories of men and women who did "live like that", people who as they waited for God's story to unfold, many who waited in difficult circumstances and troubling confusion, tracked in line with God's relational plan no matter the required cost. One of those persons is Moses, an ageless first-rate example of what it means to wait eagerly for tomorrow while living faithfully today.

A first observation: his final forty years of life in God's service make it clear that the call on us to wait for what God will only do when Jesus returns is no license for indulgence now. *No Christian is waiting as God intends us to wait who is interested in nothing more satisfying than living comfortably, successfully and prosperously in this distressing world as they wait for an even more comfortable, successful, and prosperous life to live in a world remade by Jesus.*

Moses was no dawdler, no shiftless retiree from Egypt. After leaving his position as prince under Pharaoh, he settled in Midian and raised a family providing for them by tending sheep. By local standards in that day, it could be argued that in some measure during those forty years in Midian he led a relatively comfortable if not prosperous life. And it is true that when God called Moses to a decidedly uncomfortable and unprosperous existence, as He did with Jeremiah, Moses resisted, as did Jeremiah. But neither relented from God's call on their lives. Moses turned away neither from God nor from God's arduous plan for his life.

Moses recognized a higher call than to live as comfortably as possible in this world. As we will see in the next two chapters, his awareness of a call to look forward to a reward greater than was available in this life began at age forty. During his forty years in Egypt, whatever sense Moses had that he belonged with his enslaved people, perhaps as their emancipator, crystallized when he chose to leave his royal position in Egypt and to eventually exchange it for leading two million Hebrew slaves into the freedom of the wilderness and on to the Promised Land.

It seems clear to me, even clearer now that I'm in my mid-seventies, that God's calling on His followers today, post the crucifixion of

His Son, centers on waiting for Christ's return to this disordered world, and putting *all* our hope on what is certain, that Christ will restore beautiful order to this world and to our lives. And furthermore, we are to regard this period of waiting, from our birth to either our death or the Second Coming, as a privileged and welcome opportunity to delight the God who loved us at infinite cost. How? By surrendering gladly to His Spirit's present work of forming us to relate like Jesus.

Active Waiting

There is no greater call on a Christian's life than to wait for the Lord's return and in so doing to value the Spirit's work in us and through us until Jesus comes back, nor one so commonly dismissed as something to think about later. Peter doesn't give us that option. It is *now,* Peter said, that we are to wait, for what? "… to share in his (God's) eternal glory by means of Christ Jesus." And Peter insisted that we are to wait in the confidence that "after you have suffered for a little while," a little while that seems long to our time-bound awareness, "he will restore, support, and strengthen you, and he will place you on a firm foundation" that will enable us to persevere (1 Peter 5:10 NLT)[4]. No sandy foundation of promised comfort now, but instead a foundation on a rock that keeps us stable and steady in our pursuit of growing into the likeness of Jesus, even while life's storms rage inside and around us. I hear Peter telling me this:

> *I am to never passively wait for the Lord's return as an after thought, with no more valued ambition than to enjoy the good things available now in this world. To live with no infinitely broader perspective than to live*

inbetween my birth and my death is to live a wasted life, a life that fails to tell God's Larger Story by how I relate.

Moses did not passively wait! But neither did he *aggressively wait.* His first goal was not to quickly improve life's conditions for God's people. It was rather to lead them into yielded cooperation with God's agenda for their lives. Aggressive waiting is not what God had in mind for His Old Testament followers nor for Christians now who are supremely blessed to live inbetween Christ's Cross and His Coming.

To live with preeminent zeal wrapped up in changing the world is to foolishly and pointlessly usurp the Lord's prerogative. Jesus is the one who announced that when He returns, "I am making everything new" (Revelation 21:5 NLT)[5]. I don't want to be misunderstood. I am *not* saying it is wrong for Christians to feed the hungry, house the homeless, supply fresh water where it is in short supply, provide wheelchairs for the lame and bicycles for quicker transportation in poor villages, or build hospitals providing both medical professionals and modern medicine in areas with little to no health care. All the above is good and worthwhile and compassionate. I *am* saying we are to do good in this world, not only practically but morally, to oppose abortion and stand for marriage between a man and woman, among other virtuous activities.

But when our zeal for living is centered in such causes we obscure the greater and more challenging call to *relationally* relate with others, with kindness and sacrificial love that is willing to suffer, to relate with vision for who we all can become when God's love flows into our souls and out of us into the souls of others. As that ongoingly happens, we learn to "constantly be giving careful attention to one another for the purpose of stimulating one another to love and good works" (Hebrews 10:24, Kenneth Wuest translation)[6].

Back now to Moses. He was not an aggressive socially progressive zealot. Yes, with God's power he did provide water in a barren wilderness. And yes, on his watch and under his supervision, Israel ate bread that came down from heaven. But through all the ups and downs, mostly downs, of living for forty years in an inhospitable wilderness with mostly hard-to-lead Hebrew people, Moses never quit. He faithfully, not perfectly but resolutely, sought to shepherd God's chosen people on their journey to the Promised Land. And that is part of our call today, to mutually encourage and strengthen each other as we journey together toward home.

Moses *actively* waited for his "great reward" (see Hebrews 11:26)[7], neither *passively* nor *aggressively* waiting for a reward that came after his death. And that is God's call to Christians today, to actively wait for tomorrow as we live to love well today. The call is announced in Scripture. Consider the following five verses, chosen from many others with the same message.

—

"Wait patiently for the Lord. Be brave and courageous" (Psalm 27:14 NLT)[8]: active waiting with patience as troubles continue and dreams shatter, neither passive nor aggressive waiting. We're to wait bravely and courageously, knowing our waiting takes place on a sometimes treacherous, often disappointing narrow road. As we wait for our great reward, we're to remain active in advancing the script of God's Larger Story, doing our part in becoming relationally formed into "little Christs", Jesus followers who put His love on display by how we relate, encouraging each other to discover the joy of loving well as we move along on a difficult journey.

"Wait for the Lord and keep his way" (Psalm 37:34 ESV)[9]. We're to wait for the Lord to bring human history to a close, to unfold eternity in a fashion that deepens God's delight as He gives us our keenly anticipated great reward, life with Him, literally, face-to-face, in a world of unspoiled beauty and no danger. Until then we're to actively keep His way, to "go and make disciples" (Matthew 28:19 NLT)[10], our Lord's final command to His followers before He ascended into the Father's world. Under inspiration, Paul adds this: "Live wisely among those who are not believers. And make the most of every opportunity" (Colossians 4:5 NLT)[11]. Opportunity for what? I presume evangelism. But one thing is clear. We are not to *centrally* arrange for personal comfort and felt well-being, nor are we to aggressively charge ahead with the priority of changing and improving culture. We're to wait for *then* and keep His way *now*.

"It is good that one should wait quietly for the salvation of the Lord" (Lamentations 3:26 ESV)[12]. Perhaps in this verse there is no clearer statement of the Lord's desire that we are to wait in difficult circumstances without yielding to the temptation to prioritize making a hard life easier. As I write those words, I'm sitting in a hospital infusion ward with chemotherapy dripping into my vein to fight against leukemia. I sincerely and deeply want my hard life to be easier. The question is, do I want something more? Do I want to delight God by how I relate to the medical staff whether the chemo works or not?

The words quoted above from Lamentations were written by Jeremiah, the weeping prophet who had abundant reason to weep. His encouraging words were written to citizens of Judah in the wake of Babylon's destruction of their nation.

Neither slacking off in resigned defeatism nor aggressively fighting for justice was called for by the prophet. Through Jeremiah, God was calling Judah's freshly enslaved citizens to faithful activity, to "Build homes and plan to stay" in a land that was not their home (Jeremiah 29:5 NLT)[13], to trust God for His promised but not yet granted deliverance as they lived in the ongoing reality of heartbreaking desolation. The call is clear:

> *Wait for tomorrow. Demand nothing today. But enjoy God's blessings today. And yet, whether in blessings or trials, live to love well today.*

"We ourselves eagerly wait for the hope of righteousness" (Galatians 5:5 ESV)[14]. In these words I hear the call to be "certain that God, who began the good work" in each of us "will continue his work *until it is finally finished on the day when Christ returns.*" (Philippians 1:6 NLT; emphasis mine)[15]. Paul is passionately urging us to actively cooperate with the Spirit now, before Jesus returns; to tag along with Him as He goes about His plan to form us like Jesus little by little until the day of glorious completion when Christ returns and we see Him and are then wonderfully changed. Again the point is made: wait neither passively nor aggressively but actively, keeping in step with God's Spirit.

"… you turned to God from idols…" and you resolved "to wait for his Son from heaven" (1 Thessalonians 1:9 ESV)[16]. Whatever carries us away from God and toward our smaller story, the story lived inbetween our birth and our death, is an idol. When resting in God's love is mistakenly understood to mean passivity in God service, then entitled easy going in hopes for a pleasant life becomes an idol.

When godly ministry morphs into zealous resolve to improve this culture, a resolve giving top priority to make life in this world more comfortable, prosperous, and fair, and even more moral, turns missional work into an idol. Mission trips to build homes, churches, and hospitals are good; they honor the Lord's compassion for impoverished communities, but the quality of relationships among the missionaries and with the locals delights Him even more. It puts the relational nature of Jesus on display. Remember we are exhorted to give careful attention to one another in order to stimulate one another, *first* to love, *then* to good works (see Hebrews 10:24)[17].

We best worship our relational trinitarian God by actively yielding to the Holy Spirit's slow and sometimes painful work of spiritually, relationally, forming our hearts, souls, and minds, as we eagerly wait for Jesus to bring social justice into a new heaven and a new earth. It is then, not before, that in the midst of unblemished beauty saved people will live in the uncorrupted image of Christ forever in happily productive and always restful community, an eternity worth waiting for.

Reflect on these five and other similar passages in Scripture and God's call become clear:

We're to *actively* wait for the Lord's return, to wait neither *passively* nor *aggressively*.

—

Moses followed that call. Four decades of living in the passive enjoyment of Egyptian luxury failed to satisfy his restlessly thirsty soul. And aggressively trying to bring some measure of justice to his God-chosen but wrongly enslaved people was important to him, but Moses embraced a higher call, to delight God by remaining faithful to God's mysterious plan for Moses and God's people.

At age forty, now shaped by God to realize that no eternal good came either from passively waiting for God in comfort or from aggressively waiting with ill-timed effort to make external circumstances better for God's people, Moses was prepared to make life-changing decisions. Once those decisions were made, Moses was led by God into the second four decades of his life, actively waiting for whatever God had in mind as he tended to his family and work, waiting to live into his eternally significant destiny.

Look with me now at remarkable evidence of developing maturity in Moses at age forty, maturity that prepared him at age eighty to set out on the final four decades of his life, difficult decades of actively waiting for his great reward as he remained faithful to his call.

CHAPTER FIVE

Moses Waited!

In his classic book *Holiness*[1], J. C. Ryle draws several insightful lessons from the end of the first forty-year season in the life of Moses. And he draws them from three pregnant verses written by the writer to the Hebrews. Each lesson, recorded by Ryle in 1877, is worth a fresh look. Together they paint a winning portrait of a God-follower who waited.

Here are the three verses:

"By faith Moses, when he was grown up, refused to be called the son of Pharaoh's daughter, choosing rather to be mistreated with the people of God than to enjoy the fleeting pleasures of sin. He considered the reproach of Christ greater wealth than the treasures of Egypt, for he was looking forward to the reward" (Hebrews 11:24-26 ESV; some translations have "great reward")[2].

What Moses turned from and turned to is remarkable, counter-intuitive, and completely out of step with culture, both ancient and modern.

Notice what Moses *turned from*.

FROM POSITION

First, Moses gave up a guaranteed-for-life place of power and prestige as a prince of Egypt. He did so for one reason: because of his faith that God had something better in mind for him.

Pharaoh's daughter had not only rescued the infant Moses out of an improvised, raft-like carriage floating in the Nile River (the story is told in Exodus 2:1-10)[3], but she also adopted him as her son. If several history scholars are correct, Moses was her only child and therefore positioned to rise to prominence in Pharaoh's court, perhaps even to be first in line to his grandfather's throne. Power and prestige were his for the taking.

Imagine a young person primed to lead a Fortune 400 company or to be signed to a multi-million dollar contract by a top ranked professional sports team or perhaps to lead a prominent mega church and to inevitably develop a nationally recognized voice in the Christian culture. Of course nothing would be wrong, though likely risky, in accepting any one of those powerful and prestigious opportunities - unless God was calling the young person elsewhere, perhaps to a relational lifestyle that would be interfered with by any of the understandably attractive opportunities just mentioned. If a call elsewhere became clear to the young person, imagine the compelling strong temptation to convince himself or herself that a good and loving God would never lead someone so gifted and sought after to a "lesser" opportunity.

Hebrews tells us that when he was "grown up", now forty years old, it was "by faith" that Moses "refused to be called the son of Pharaoh's daughter", thus renouncing all his privileges, exchanging his identity as a prince in a royal household for a brother of an enslaved people. Moses honored a higher calling on his life, but at that time knowing only that he would identify himself as a slave among slaves, similar to a calling to Christians today to be slaves of Jesus Christ heading toward a glory-filled destiny.

No psychologist should be listened to who would suggest that Moses was diagnosable as a self-hating masochist, preferring poverty and misery to wealth and comfort. The following eighty years in Moses' life, particularly the final forty, make it clear that he, a resolute worshiper of God, was waiting for God's best, knowing the narrow road journey meant hardship first, then glory.

Through to his last breath before death, Moses believed that there was nothing better than the reward prepared for him by God, even when his natural life ended in severe disappointment. Moses died *looking* at the Promised Land, never *entering* it. And yet he died still shepherding God's people, blessing them as they, without him, prepared to cross over Jordan into Canaan.

Moses stands as both a rebuke and an encouragement to Christians today. When we resolutely pursue a satisfactory life style for ourselves with no serious thought given to what kind of life God might be calling us, we reveal that we are addicted, perhaps not to alcohol or porn, but to personal comfort, to quenching a thirst woefully less than a thirst to know God and to make Him known to others by the way we relate. We find ourselves addicted to a source of happiness other than God Himself, other than the inestimable privilege, though a costly one, of joining His Larger Story. We turn away from God's best for our lives, refusing to wait for the day when His difficult best will be validated as indeed having been the best way to live.

By example, Moses tells us that to turn away from falsely coveted power and prestige, from pride-strengthening ability to influence the affairs of this world, knowing God is calling us to a different path to soul satisfaction, is to live free, as a slave to God. By faith, with chosen trust that breeds confidence that God's way really is best, Moses waited.

FROM PLEASURE

Second, we're told in Hebrews that Moses "refused the fleeting pleasures of sin".

What would persuade and empower an addict to refuse the temporary but overwhelmingly satisfying indulgence of a strong appetite for pleasure-providing sin? In another chapter I will wrestle with that question. For now, I want us to notice that Moses did what seems impossible to many, to refuse "the fleeting pleasures of sin". No doubt the bigwigs in the Egyptian government exercised little such restraint. They were not limited in their pursuit of most any pleasure that struck their fancy, including sex and drink. As a younger adult, before he was "grown up", did Moses seize the opportunities for such pleasure? It seems so. The writer to the Hebrews inspired by God's Spirit, lets us know that *as a middle aged-man* Moses refused those fleeting pleasures. Does that detail imply that during earlier years he had not refused them?

One of the devil's most insidiously compelling strategies is to turn us away from God and toward sin by deluding us into thinking, if only at a critical moment of decision, that sexual pleasure, perhaps a drug induced buzz, or some other available route to immediate comfort will satisfy the thirst we most long to quench. In order to pull off this deception, Satan, with devilish wisdom, works to never let us discover, especially in that critical moment, the human thirst alive in our inmost being that can be touched with true joy only from knowing God's love well enough to want to pass it on to others.

But the joy available only as the fruit of the Spirit's work within us is never complete, at least not for long. An ache remains. A battle between sin and holiness rages on within us. Fear, hurt feelings, anxiety, a nagging sense of guilt are never entirely dissipated. Uncertainty about the future continues to heckle us. We long for relief from all those concerns. And that is the devil's trump card. The pleasure brought by our favorite addiction provides that relief, if only briefly, seemingly requiring that we revert to indulging an addictive pleasure when needed.

Assume that as a God-loved Hebrew, Moses' image-bearing soul longed for satisfaction that the fleeting pleasures of sin always available in Egypt could never provide. Even so, the temptations were great. Think what pleasures were his to enjoy from his early days to age forty: the intoxicating pleasures of sex, the numbing power of strong drink, the attractiveness of fine clothes, the felt pride of deference from less important people, the unmatched comfort of richly appointed living quarters, the head turning when Moses rode out in the latest model chariot driven by well groomed and decorated horses, and the proud delight of enjoying regular access to Pharaoh and his favor, as well as to the best available medical care. All these pleasures and more were at the disposal of Prince Moses.

But can we suppose that God's Spirit, anticipating the script written in heaven for the life of Moses, penetrated into the untouched and unawakened regions of his soul, introducing Moses to the exhaustion of unsatisfied desire? Was Moses being prepared to realize that every source of good feelings available to him in the world of Egypt were nothing more than fleeting pleasures? Pleasures wrongly experienced as soul satisfying delights? Addictions worthy of neither celebration nor continued indulgence?

Supernatural discernment was needed for Moses to recognize that such fleeting pleasures were a snare, not a blessing; delights that warred against his soul. God was at work, shaping Moses to embrace his destiny as He is in each of our lives. How sad that our lives are often too busy and too noisy to recognize the Spirit's work.

Moses came to see, as must we, that the joy he was designed to experience was found entirely in God's plan. And that joy must be God's doing. Moses waited! As must we if we are to live as true disciples of Jesus.

FROM PROSPERITY

Third, Moses turned his back on material wealth. He turned away from living high on the treasures of Egypt.

As the adopted grandson of Pharaoh, a very rich grandfather, Moses assuredly could have been like Scrooge McDuck and counted his gold every day. An overflowing bank account removed all worry of not being able to afford something he wanted. It's a good feeling, enjoyed by many in western culture, to be able to pay our bills and have money left over for dinner at a fine restaurant. Without placing all our hope in the return of Jesus, including hope for a wonderfully comfortable, worry-free existence, we would not be easily drawn to a call from God that required us to now live with less.

Folks at all levels of financial resources, from the mega wealthy to the desperate poor, would likely without compunction grab at an opportunity to acquire additional funds. Poor people want money. Rich people typically want more money. As a prince of Egypt, Moses no doubt enjoyed his wealth. Yet he exchanged riches for poverty. Why? God's call on his life required it. And Moses was "looking forward to the reward" of finding meaning and joy and friendship with God by telling His story, following God's script for his life.

It must again be noted: Moses did not turn away from his God-created longing to be happy. But he did turn away from searching for happiness in all the wrong places, including material wealth.

Apparently, Moses believed the tired but true maxim that money cannot buy happiness, at least not the happiness God designs for us to enjoy the most.

Moses turned his life in a direction that to most onlookers then and now seemed a sure route to misery. By faith and only by faith, Moses knew otherwise. Even when his time during the last forty years of his life became, by earthly measures, miserable, and no doubt felt miserable, Moses evidently remained convinced that the God he obeyed was firmly committed to the well-being of his soul. How else could he have continued waiting?

We must not miss the clear teaching of Jesus, plainly on display in the life of Moses:

> **The path to happiness, to the joy and hope-filled well-being of a Christian's soul, leads *both* through some level of affliction, weariness, and angst, sometimes to nearly unbearable levels, *and* to the awareness of a deep thirst that will be fully satisfied only in the next life, a thirst that stirs joyful, persevering hope.**

To the belief that anguish and hope are inevitable in a God-follower's life, I see Moses nodding in passionate agreement. He turned away from position, pleasure, and prosperity. He waited for a greater reward. And now he is enjoying never ending joy as he lives his life with God, in His immediate presence. Moses waited. It was a good decision.

In the next chapter we'll see not what he *turned from*, that was just discussed in this chapter, but what he *turned to*. Moses chose to live his life on what Jesus called the narrow road.

CHAPTER SIX

Foolish Choices

Still borrowing from J.C. Ryle's discerning observations about the life of Moses as recorded in Hebrews 11: 24-26[1], we can identify three foolish *appearing* choices that Moses made at age forty that led him from the luxury of Egypt to the bleak land of Midian. If there is no Larger Story to tell, if the smaller story lived inbetween our birth and our death is all there is, then his choices were indeed foolish. But – believe the Bible's teaching that God is telling a great story that began in eternity past and will last forever in eternity future, and these same choices make perfect sense. Obedience to God always does. The choices Moses made provided him with a meaningful if difficult life and put him on a path to his destiny of a great reward.

Drawing from Ryle, in the previous chapter I suggested that Moses *turned away* from power, pleasure, and prosperity, three opportunities to lead the good life as understood by most. In this chapter I want us to see that Moses *turned to* three paths pretty well guaranteed to make his life formidable, difficult, and wearisome. Looking into his life as revealed in our Hebrews passage, we can recognize that though formidable, difficult, and wearying, the life Moses led told the story God had scripted for him. In retrospect, his three choices were wise.

TO SUFFERING

First, Moses chose suffering, misfortune, and abuse, or as Hebrews puts it, he *chose* mistreatment.

Moses made his first choice knowing that Pharaoh, his adoptive grandfather, would not be happy. He sided with a Hebrew slave against an Egyptian citizen. He killed the Egyptian who was "beating one of his fellow Hebrews" (Exodus 2: 11 NLT)[2]. Moses wanted to defend and protect his people, the people chosen of God. It is possible, I think likely, that Moses thought he was taking his first step in liberating the Hebrews from slavery, thinking that as a prince in Egypt he was qualified to do the job. When he killed the Egyptian though, he must have expected to be mistreated by Pharaoh. He did not, however, expect to be mistreated by the people he was trying to help. But he was.

Pharaoh felt severely betrayed by the man who had enjoyed prosperous living, good food, and an excellent education, all provided by Egypt. He now wanted to kill the grandson who was likely in line to succeed Pharaoh as King. I doubt if Pharaoh's intention surprised Moses.

But I do not doubt that he expected support from his Hebrew brothers, and perhaps also from God. Neither came his way. The day after he killed the Egyptian, Moses attempted to put a stop to a fight he stumbled into going on between two Hebrews. Rather reasonably, he asked the man who had started the fight, "Why are you beating up your friend" (Exodus 2: 13 NLT)[3]? That man replied, "Who appointed you to be our prince and judge. Are you going to kill me as you killed the Egyptian yesterday" (Exodus 2: 2: 14 NLT)[4]?

His self-chosen task to free the Jews from slavery and to help them get along was off to a bad start. It went downhill from there.

Forty years later, Moses was living with Israel in the wilderness, leading them to the Promised Land. Many of the Israelites were complaining about the hard conditions. "Moses heard all the families standing in the doorways of their tents whining…" (Numbers 11: 10 NLT)[5]. Their whining really got to Moses. He cried out to the Lord, "The load is far too heavy. If this is how you intend to treat me" now that I'm doing what you told me to do, "just go ahead and kill me. Do me a favor and spare me this misery" (Numbers 11: 14 NLT)[6]. Pharaoh wanted Moses dead years earlier. Now Moses felt mistreated not only by his fellow Jews but by the God he was serving.

Scores of today's Christians feel similarly. The world, typified by Pharaoh, opposes Christianity in increasing measure. Fellow believers in church sometimes treat other believers in ways we commonly call abuse. And God, allegedly speaking through the church, seems to offer little in dealing with the very real problems some Christians experience. Mistreatment from the world; from fellow Christians in the church, often Christians in leadership; and apparently from God; it's enough to turn Christians off to conventional Christianity.

On a "chance encounter" some time ago, I met a man who asked me if I still believed what I'd written in my books. I replied yes, and then asked the reason for his obviously challenging question. Immediately and with some belligerence, he answered: "I used to believe all that Christian stuff about shattered dreams leading to joy by a God who always means us good. I even taught Sunday school and served as an elder in my church. But God refused to answer one prayer that meant the world to me. My fellow elders encouraged me to wait on the Lord to see what good would eventually come. It didn't. I'll tell you this: if God exists, He isn't worth trusting. I'm done with Christianity, church and Christians."

Some turn away more quietly. Some, like this man, quite obviously.

I wonder: had Moses known what was coming, would he have chosen a path that would lead to suffering, such mistreatment and abuse, with so little apparent help from God? Jesus told us that the road He wants us to take through life is narrow, and the word narrow means troubled, afflicted. Would I have chosen to heed Christ's call to walk the narrow road if I had known how narrow the road could become? Do I sometimes feel more *stuck* with Christianity than *grateful* for knowing Jesus as Savior and wanting to follow Him?

Old age is now upon me. Could abundant hardships as time continues lead me to forsake all hope of living an abundant life of loving God and others till I die, of finishing well? Will I eagerly wait for what lies ahead when Jesus returns? Will I remain faithful until then?

As always, Jesus is our example, our compassionate High Priest who "understands our weaknesses, for he faced all of the same testings we do, yet he did not sin" (Hebrews 4: 15 NLT)[7]. Until Gethsemane, even our Lord did not fully realize how terribly He would suffer. Calvary made it exquisitely clear. *And yet Jesus waited!* He knew what lay ahead, after His resurrection, after His ascension, after several thousand years of church and world history, when He would return to make everything new.

Every Christian who demonstrates his or her faith in God by persevering, every Christian who waits for tomorrow committed to living faithfully today will in some measure be blessed by the "privilege of suffering" for Christ (Philippians 1: 29 NLT)[8]. Is any privilege less desired? Less welcomed? Will we endure? Will we wait in hope of the glory to come? Waiting is not easy.

When Peter was approaching the end of his life, he told us that there is "wonderful joy ahead, even though you must endure many trials for a little while" (I Peter 1: 6 NLT)[9]. What Peter thought of as a little while can seem like a long while to us. Two truths will help us gain perspective that a long difficult season of life can be viewed as both welcomed and short. One, when we think of our lives as lived inbetween the Cross and the Coming, not merely inbetween our birth and our death, our years spent as broken people in a broken world can be accurately seen as truly short when compared with eternal life. It is then that life as fully healed people in a fully healed world begins, when Jesus returns. And two, we can trust that God's Spirit is always doing eternally significant work in our souls, even during the worst of our "little while".

By faith, Moses fixed his hope, not on how well his wilderness wanderings went, but on a great reward that would be his to enjoy, during one eternal day. He was confident that eventually God would bless him with what he most wanted, with what his soul most desired. Moses waited! He knew what he was most thirsty for.

TO SOCIAL OUTCASTS

Second, Moses *chose* the company of a despised and broken people.

Even today, centuries later, the Jews in modern Israel are despised. One nation in particular is hell bent on their destruction. In the time of Moses, Israel was a captive people in a land where they were treated as mere chattel. Yet Moses chose to leave his place in a royal household to be with a nation of ragamuffin slaves. Even after forty years of living away from them in relative ease, Moses returned to his people at God's command and remained with them during forty more years filled with opposition from without and rebellion from within. Moses chose a difficult life.

And it was hard on him. At least once he lost his temper. Israel's water supply ran out. "The people blamed Moses and said, '...why have you brought the congregation of the Lord's people to die...? Why did you make us leave Egypt and bring us here to this terrible place?'" (Numbers 20: 3-5 NLT)[10]. God then told Moses to "speak to the rock over there, and it will pour out its water" (Number 20: 8 NLT)[11]. Earlier God had said to strike a rock when water was needed. This time Moses disobeyed. He was fed up. "Listen, you rebels!" 'he shouted'. "Must we bring you water from this rock? Then Moses raised his hand and struck the rock twice with his staff, and water gushed out'" (Numbers 20: 10-11 NLT)[12]. I think I can almost hear Moses then shouting again: "There! Go ahead and drink, you sniveling complainers." Venting can feel so good in the moment.

But neither uncontrolled venting nor disobedience to a specific command from God was his pattern. Even though his self-control wavered in that moment, Moses was not addicted, as so many Christians today are, to feeling good. He kept ministering to people who everyday annoyed him, simply because God wanted him to do so. Moses waited for tomorrow while remaining faithful today.

We still sometimes remark, a person is known by the company he keeps. By that standard, the choice Moses made to live in the company of stiff-necked Jews made him a fool, a man who made a foolish choice. And a fool he was, *if and only if there is but one life to live, and if no better life awaits us after death.*

That choice seems even more foolish knowing that he spent the final forty years of his life, from age eighty to one hundred twenty, the so-called "golden years", leading irritating people to a wonderful land that Moses never entered. From a "birth to death" perspective, Moses should have stayed in Egypt, perhaps using his position and resources to lighten the load of the Hebrew slaves. Instead, he waited! Today, he has no regrets.

TO SCORN

Third, Moses chose reproach and rebuke; he *chose* personally humiliating suffering.

Imagine what his Egyptian friends and colleagues might have said to Moses when they heard that he killed an Egyptian and was preparing to flee *alone* to Midian. "What a stupid thing you did. You're leaving the comforts of life here in Pharaoh's court because you aligned yourself with a mere Hebrew slave, and against one of Pharaoh's subjects? You idiot! You've risked your life and are now heading to some nowhere place. Moses, have you lost your mind?" Moses would likely have been shamed by such words as he hurriedly packed a few things planning to run away before Pharaoh's soldiers found and killed him.

From earliest days, every child fears the humiliating reproach of others. Though better hidden by adults, the same fear remains throughout our lives. We do what we can to blunt the impact of shame, brought on perhaps by our own stupid choices. But still it hurts, deeply. Loving others as Christ loves us too often takes a back seat to protecting ourselves from relational pain.

Too often we conform to the expectations of others whose respect we assume we need for self respect. It is a rare person so centered in God's love that reproach is perhaps difficult to handle but not devastating at some deep internal level. To a substantial degree, Moses was that rare person.

Jesus endured far more than Moses ever experienced: three years of apparently failed ministry; agony in Gethsemane exacerbated by three close friends falling asleep; beatings and derision in Pilate's courtyard; the unmatched horror of Calvary accompanied by gross spitting, sarcastic laughter, cruel taunting, and malicious mocking, all endured without complaint, only forgiving love directed toward His abusers. No call to twelve legions of angels was spoken. Jesus waited, knowing neither the reproach nor rebuke denied His identity as the Son of God. And He knew what His suffering would accomplish when He rose, ascended to heaven, and came back to rule over the earth.

If only in this life of thirty-three years He had hope in His Father, Jesus would have been worthy of little more than pity, a martyr for no enduring purpose. But Jesus never lost confidence that a story of fathomless love, matchless goodness, and stunning mercy was unfolding. He believed the climax would be worth the cost. Jesus waited!

As did Moses. But it is true that when God finally called him to his earthly destiny, this time to successfully rescue Israel from Egypt and lead the chosen people to the Promised Land, Moses resisted, in fear. Had God emptied Moses of the proud confidence he must have felt when as an important person in Egypt he appointed himself to free Israel? Had forty years in Midian worn him down, helped him to feel inadequate for so great a task? Apparently so. Only the emptiness of self, the loss of pride, releases us to receive fullness of soul as we undertake His business.

At God's urging, including His anger, Moses obeyed. The burning bush changed everything. In God's power, Moses led the people out of Egypt, across the Red Sea, and on to Mt. Sinai. Then? Forty years wandering in the wilderness with people who refused to give him the honor he deserved as God's choice to lead them to Canaan. I wonder how many pastors can relate?

Moses endured. He waited. But if the hope of leading the people not only *to* Canaan but *into* the Promised Land sustained his long perseverance, he was sorely disappointed. Because Moses struck the rock when he was told to speak to it, God denied him that privilege. Shattered dreams can make faithful perseverance especially difficult. But Moses *still* waited.

Still outside of Canaan shortly before his death, "Moses the man of God" pronounced "a blessing" on Israel as without him they would soon march into Canaan (see Deuteronomy 33:1)[13]. No doubt Moses was waiting *both* in sorrow over disappointment *and* in hope of a greater reward yet to come: a wonderful picture of what it means to wait.

And that, I suggest, is God's call to each of us, to resist quitting on obedience and on arranging for our own relief and pleasure when life gets rough. With resolve fueled by faith, we are to wait for the Lord's return, with even greater fervency when our dreams for this life shatter. Waiting for the Second Coming can go a long way in helping us quit looking for pleasurable relief as an entitled pursuit. Relief is coming. And joy forever.

Whether we are meaningfully waiting for the Lord's return to console our inconsolable longing; whether we refuse to wait but instead provide ourselves with moments, perhaps seasons, of sadness-numbing satisfaction now; or whether we're foolish enough to think current blessings reduce the need to wait; and therefore never come to grips with our ever present addiction to self;

Moses points to what is possible: to wait!

We must follow his lead, more particularly the lead of Jesus. We must wait. But a question begs an answer:

What needs to go on within us that will empower us to wait? Read on.

PART II

DIFFICULT WAITING

It's Possible

CHAPTER SEVEN

The Struggle for Self-Control

You've read Part I. Now for Part II, the hard part. In Part I, I've already convinced myself, and hopefully you, that the Bible is the source of my belief that waiting with passionate anticipation for the Lord's return is necessary, but perhaps not sufficient, for gaining meaningful self-control over our addictive urges. The "perhaps" phrase is important. In my own battle against the perils of addiction, I'm realizing two things: *first,* the battle never ends; the flesh never dies. And *second,* other God-provided resources complement waiting in empowering Christians to resist seemingly irresistible temptations.

Now it must be noted: the self-control I'm after, a power available only through the Holy Spirit, not only resists temptation but also releases divinely accessed love into our way of relating. Other means of gaining self-control run the risk of promoting satisfaction with one's own unaided moral success, which stirs nothing of the anticipated pleasure of loving someone else more than the self-righteous enjoyment of loving one's own virtuous achievements.

Passionately active waiting for the Second Coming has real

present and practical value, both to resist sinful urges and to release godly relating. But is such eager waiting for that great event truly possible? It seems that waiting for anything we want to come our way, anything that brings even a moment of sadness-numbing pleasure, anything that dulls the ever present ache of unsatisfied desire in our souls, is difficult. It's hard enough for me, a self-confessed coffee addict, to patiently wait for a cup of the hot brew to be served when I sit down at a restaurant's breakfast table. Waiting for a second cup while the server is busy elsewhere is even more annoying. If waiting for such trivial pleasures requires effort, is patiently waiting for the Lord's "imminent" return, which though guaranteed could happen later today or a thousand years from now, really possible? That's the central question on my mind as I write Part II.

Let me prepare for Part II by briefly repeating the response I gave to the question addressed in Part I: does waiting for then have real value for now?

Waiting for Jesus would prove useful, I believe essential, in slowly and significantly overcoming our universal addiction to self, to self-centeredness, to what I think of as relational sin, to the depravity that lies at the root of our wide variety of specific addictions, each one a symptom of our self-serving nature which refuses to die.

That brief summary of Part I turned into one long sentence. To prevent my wordiness from being heard as an undecipherable mumble, some clarification seems in order. My contention that waiting for the Second Coming has real value in resisting addictive urges is built on one two-part assumption. Regrettably, the key assumption beneath my thinking is unpopular, an assumption most often either strongly disputed or quickly and cavalierly dismissed.

The first half of my assumption: the *proximate* cause of whatever addiction we struggle against has less to do with neurological or chemical malfunction in the brain and more to do with our demand for felt relief from the inconsolable ache of a never fully satisfied, always still thirsty soul.

The *root* cause lies deeper. The demand for felt relief that is under our control, that requires no waiting, only a choice, emerges from the God-dishonoring swamp of our justified sense of entitlement to satisfaction when desired. When God doesn't come through on our timetable, we claim the right to provide for our satisfaction. That swamp is what the Bible calls our flesh, the old nature we inherited as Adam's progeny. Too many treatments for addictive disorders do little more than socialize the flesh, perhaps achieving long term sobriety for addicts, but leaving them no less controlled by their entitled nature, now only in less obviously destructive ways. That the root cause of addiction lies in our self-centered nature is the second half of my assumption.

Another nature, a loving other-centered nature that can successfully compete with one's self-centered nature, is therefore required both for resistance to addictive urges and for the release of love, setting the recovering addict on the path to relational holiness. We need a new nature not only to love well but also even to envision what loving well involves and to desire to pay the daily price to love well.

The new nature supplied by God's Spirit to everyone who trusts Jesus for forgiveness from sin comes with the opportunity of living today with hope for tomorrow, for the Lord's promised return. We then become capable of living in the presence of God, knowing Him now, waiting for Him then. When death from advanced incurable cancer was imminent, despite the prayers of thousands for miraculous healing, Francis Schaeffer, the great Christian apologist of the late 1900's, was asked by a friend what he was thinking. He replied, "When you're in the presence of God, it's unbecoming to demand anything."[1]

He died three weeks later, his comment the words of a waiting saint, spoken from his new nature.

But perhaps it is possible to wait only when death is near. Could it be that only then our longing for heaven would be strong enough to effectively compete with any demand for whatever little satisfaction is still available in this world? Is that true? Is it possible to eagerly wait for the next life with apparently at least some years still left before we die?

That's the question we must face. Waiting for certain and complete satisfaction when Jesus returns or when we die would provide real *value* in resisting the appeal of yielding now to addictive opportunities for relief. It's the *possibility* of waiting earnestly and eagerly enough to release forces within us powerful enough to compete with the lure of addictive pleasures that is now the question.

CHAPTER EIGHT

Is Self-Control Possible? It Depends!

Suppose we had a clear command in the Bible declared by God that read as follows:

"I instruct you to wait for the Second Coming of My Son with great passion. My Spirit will then use that passion to provide you with the power to resist temptation to sin. I now command you: **Wait with great passion!**"

How would I obey that command? Could I produce passion by an act of my will deciding to call it up? Are emotions under my direct volitional control? Can anyone simply choose to *feel* great passion about something, even something as climactic as the Second Coming?

One Sunday morning during my fourth year in elementary school, my Sunday school teacher told us how we could learn to say no to sin and yes to God. A simple technique would generate the passion to do the right thing. His advice was this: "When you feel an urge to do something you know you shouldn't do, picture two dogs, a good dog and a bad one. In your mind's eye look at the good dog, point him to the bad dog and say 'sic him'. You will then feel a stronger urge to do good. Remember, which dog you say 'sic him' to will be the dog you obey."

His advice made sense to me, then. In school the next day, the teacher surprised us with an unscheduled spelling test. She would slowly announce a word and we would spell it on our test papers. I wasn't prepared, but no matter. I was a good speller. Lyle and I were recognized as the two best spellers in our class. I wasn't worried. But soon she gave out a word I wasn't certain how to correctly spell. I felt great passion to get it right.

Lyle was sitting next to me, a mere foot away in our crowded classroom. I glanced his way and saw him spelling the difficult word with no hesitation. An urge rose up in me to sneak another peak at his paper, long enough to see how he spelled that one word. I wanted to cheat. I wanted to keep up with Lyle. I felt no desire, only obligation, to *not* cheat, to risk making a mistake on the spelling test.

I remembered my Sunday school teacher's advice, a way to feel passion to do the right thing. With deliberate firmness, I told the good dog to sic the bad dog. It didn't work. I felt nothing, no new desire to be good. I still wanted to cheat. But I did feel a trace of guilt. I therefore delivered an even stronger command: "Good dog, sic that bad dog". Again, nothing. I felt only one great passion, to spell every word correctly.

I waited till the teacher looked down, then I looked over at Lyle's paper, saw what I assumed was the proper spelling and wrote it on my paper. When the test was complete, the teacher then gave the correct spelling for each word as we graded our papers. I had them all right. On the top of my test paper, I proudly wrote 100%. Lyle missed one word. I saw him write 95% on his paper. I felt good. We turned our tests in to the teacher. Within minutes she publicly identified me as the best speller in fourth grade. I had yielded to my great passion for success. I couldn't work up a greater competitive passion to do the right thing.

Addictive urges present themselves to us with alluring passion. Telling an addict to *do* the right thing whether or not you experience a *desire* to do the right thing, is not helpful. White-knuckle efforts to resist sinful urges rarely work. And when they do? Not for long, not often as a new pattern of right choices. Worse, the mere effort to do right, supported only by moral obligation rather than by deep passion, when successful generates pride. But it must be noted: the passion needed to obey God and resist sin is felt not as an exciting feeling but rather as a usually quiet but relentless thirst. It's the thirst that we must know is in us. It is in every Christian.

The passion of a thirst to do right in order to delight God and to claim our privileged part in His larger story is necessary if the Holy Spirit is to play His part in empowering obedience. Spirit-empowered obedience then generates awed gratitude for His role in our lives.

If God were to command me to wait for His Son's return with great passion, with greater passion than for my life to move along smoothly, without an awareness of a living thirst for what only God makes possible in my life both now in this present world and then in the next world, I would be at a loss. I'd throw in the towel and conclude obedience to that command is not possible. To conclude otherwise requires that we explore what it means to live thirsty, thirsty for God as we live in the complexities and concerns of daily life.

I just now took a break from writing to call a specialty doctor, wanting to schedule an unpleasant treatment for the cancer still in my body. I left a message. I want the procedure scheduled soon so I can move past it into better health. Am I right now *most* compellingly thirsty for the Lord's return or for the doctor's phone call? Truth be told, I feel more passionately eager for the phone to ring than to hear the voice of the archangel shouting "Christ returns!". I long to hear that voice but right now I'm really wanting to hear from my doctor.

If passionate waiting for tomorrow, with a passion better understood as a welcoming thirst for God to have His way, is essential for holy living today, what am I to do?

The question must be asked and at least addressed:

Is it possible to wait for the Second Coming with thirsty passion, with a passion stronger than my desire for things to go well now? And when things don't go well now, is it possible to long more for the Lord's return than either for relief from distress or for a pleasure to enjoy what is available on demand?

Is it possible? That's the question. The answer is yes. But a few other things must fall into place in order for me to become aware of the insatiable thirst that is already in me, a thirst that would stir a passionate waiting for the Second Coming. What are these "other things"?

CHAPTER NINE

Passions that Strengthen the Power to Wait

The question is bugging me: *is it possible?*

It's a pattern. Important questions are difficult to answer. Let me suggest you slowly read this chapter and the next. The answer to the above question gets tricky.

In this book, I believe I'm tackling two important questions. The first, will a Christian who waits eagerly for the Second Coming discover both compelling reason and adequate strength to better resist addictive urges? The example of Moses laid out in Part I encourages me to answer yes. Eager waiting for what lies ahead will help us say no to temptation. It works like this: **if the prospect of heaven so delights us that we demand nothing in this life, the appeal of sinful pleasure becomes resistible.**

The second question, which I think may be more important than the first one and therefore more difficult to answer, asks, is it possible? *Is it even possible for any Christian to be so drawn to the sinless holy pleasures awaiting us that sinful unholy pleasures available now lose their controlling power?*

It must be quickly admitted that nothing possible to us in this world frees us to never sin. Remember what the aged apostle John told us: "If we claim we have no sin, we are only fooling ourselves and not living in truth" (I John 1: 8 NLT)[1]. We must be honest; until we reach heaven we will have reason to repent, often, especially if we recognize our addiction to relational sin, to somehow using others for our own well-being.

Perhaps we need to rephrase question two: can we be so eager for the Lord's return that our passion for then might strengthen us, though never fully, in our present battle against sin? Notice that there is no reason to even raise this question unless we are already persuaded that eager waiting for the Second Coming will help us to more often say no to sin.

If we are so persuaded, then my second question does need to be raised: is it even possible to wait so eagerly for the Lord's coming that the prospect of actually seeing Him will fortify us against sin's appeal? We already know that no one can simply choose to feel excited about anything, even something so momentous as the Lord's return. If we're to get truly excited about our Lord coming back to make everything as it should be, we must head in a direction other than trying to work up passion for what lies ahead.

It requires no special discernment to realize that we all want something. The most honest among us admits that however much we have, our deepest thirst is never fully quenched. Too often our response to that disappointment is to numb our unsatisfied thirst and to gladly feel whatever thirst we can somehow manage to satisfy. I think that process begins in a child's earliest years.

And that's a sensible option, unless there is something available to us that awakens our deepest thirst with certain hope that it will be satisfied, in measure now, and fully forever. What then is it that we all most intensely want? What could draw out our deepest thirst and stir us with passion that it might be available?

Christians believe, at least we have reason to, that what ever it is we most long to experience is available in Christianity, and available only in Christianity. Let me broaden that claim. What every one most wants, whether Christian or not, can be found only in Christianity.

But what is it? What does Christianity alone provide that most satisfies the human soul, something that could double us over with passion for the Second Coming? The God who knows what real joy is, who experiences it fully in His three-Person community, created us to experience His joy. And all three divine Persons have gone to extreme lengths to make that joy available to us. I remember years ago teaching a Sunday school class extolling the privileges offered to us in Christianity when one man, a wealthy man with a good family, raised his hand to ask, "Where's the joy?" I had no clear answer then. I think I do, now.

What does Christianity provide that awakens our deepest, strongest, most pressing desire, that arouses a thirst like no other for what Christ came to give us? Until we know what that is, our deepest thirst will lie dormant, asleep in our souls. And then, as long as our core desire remains unawakened, we will seek satisfaction of lesser thirst in the world's resources. And those resources are considerable, able to generate the illusion of rich satisfaction, at least for a while.

We will not live the Christian life to its fullest until we recognize what Christianity offers that the human soul in its deepest regions most desires. What is it? What is the exact center of the Christian message, the incomparable good news of the Gospel of Christ? Let me offer four answers that surround the center.

It's not forgiveness of sins. Thanks to our Lord's willingness to die in our place, the death our sins deserved, we who believe are justified, fully forgiven, given the status of sons and daughters of God. As wonderful as that new identity is, it opens the door to something better.

It's not Christ's promise to return. Deny that promise and the hope of joy forever vanishes. Atheists can then supply an attractive message: get all you can today because tomorrow you'll be gone. The promise of a Second Coming is an indispensable part of Christianity's good news. But its indispensability lies not only in that glorious event, but in what it brings, full satisfaction of humanity's deepest thirst. We need to know what that is.

It's not the biblical principles that guide us through life that lie in the center of God's good news. Religious hucksters, particularly those on television, have a field day with this answer: do what you're told and life will go well. Plant a seed of one hundred dollars in someone's ministry and a hundred-fold return is guaranteed. Too many Christians believe that nonsense. Christianity does not promise earth-bound blessings to obedient people, but obedience is commanded, and sometimes does bring prayed for blessings. But obedience *always* draws us into the flow of God's Spirit. Could there be something we want more?

It's not spiritual formation. No question, the opportunity for selfish people to become selfless, like Jesus, is an undeserved and astonishing privilege. But spiritually forming Christians become capable, in this life, of enjoying a far greater privilege.

While these four things are legitimate, necessary, miraculous steps along the pathway to freedom from our self-addiction, there is something greater that lies at the center of Christianity. Once again, the question must be asked: **what is it?** What is the exact center of Christianity's good news, a center from which more good news flows? What deep thirst in you and me does Christianity meaningfully satisfy now and fully satisfy forever?

Ignore the question or answer it wrongly and you live recognizing only shallow thirst that gives Satan an opening. There is pleasure in sin, only for a season, but seasonal satisfaction of shallow desires beats permanent emptiness of soul. The stage is then set for addictions to ruin our lives. Christianity gets put aside.

But live with an awareness of our deepest thirst that nothing in this world and no other religion can satisfy, and Christianity becomes irresistible. What then is the center of Christianity that releases passion for Christ's coming, that speaks to and draws forth what the human soul most desires?

CHAPTER TEN

When the Trinity Came Alive, In Me

As a young child, I believed there was Someone named God, Someone my father prayed to at every meal. I thought it was nice to thank Him for our food, but I was with mother when she bought the food at the grocery store. In my mind, it would have made more sense for dad to turn to mother and thank her, not God, for bringing the food home then preparing it. But dad kept on thanking God for the food I was about to eat. Something strange was going on. I couldn't figure it out.

Then things got more mysterious. I learned in Sunday school that God was three Persons, a Father, a Son, and Someone else my teacher called the Holy Spirit. I remember asking my father what that was all about. He said it was true, and that all three Persons were working together to get me to heaven someday and, in the meantime, to help me be honest and good to others. I thought that was nice of them, then went out to play.

Up through my teens and into my twenties, I heard enough sermons, did enough Bible study on my own to believe, not only that the one God existed as a community of three divine Persons, but that it somehow mattered. I left it at that, finished graduate school, and began my career as a psychologist.

Somewhere along the way, I think in my late forties, I began to wonder just why the truth of the Trinity mattered, to ask how this doctrine taught in the Bible, embraced in the Apostle's Creed, and included in my church's doctrinal statement should matter to me in my daily life.

More time went by, I read books about the Trinity, and then in my fifties, I came to see that these three divine Persons, each One fully and equally God (however that worked), were telling a story that was scripted before anything was created and began to take shape in the first two chapters of Genesis, then seemed to take a left turn in Genesis three. This story, I came to understand, was designed by the Father, revealed by the Son, and was now being carried on by the Spirit.

And I realized that the plot of the story, what I then and now refer to as the Larger Story in contrast to the smaller story of my birth-to-death existence, involved people who having obtained forgiveness through the death of Jesus responded to God's amazing grace and fathomless love by loving both God and others with divine-like love, the love Jesus put on display. I could live for a purpose bigger than me, larger than my existence. I could become a teller of God's story by how I related to others, drawing them to the love of Jesus made visible in me. That mattered.

I thought I had the big picture figured out. The abundance of the abundant life Jesus said He came to give us (see John 10: 10)[1] was an abundance of the desire and ability to love made available to me in increasing measure as I became more formed like Jesus, knowing that whatever blessings came my way, and whatever trials and sorrow brought sadness and pain, were all within God's loving providence, each detail working together for my good, for the sense of personal wholeness and joyful holiness I could experience as I delighted the Father by loving like His Son.

That was a very long sentence. Let me say it again, in five shorter sentences. It's important.

- The abundance of the abundant life Jesus said He came to give us (see John 10: 10)[1] is an abundance of the desire and ability to love.
- This desire and ability to love is made available to me in increasing measure as I became more formed like Jesus.
- Whatever blessings come my way, and whatever trials and sorrow bring sadness and pain, are all within God's loving providence.
- Every blessing and sorrow would be working together for my good.
- The good result would be a sense of personal wholeness and joyful holiness I could experience as I delighted the Father by loving like His Son.

There! Case closed. The plot of the Larger Story understood. Now to live it. But how? In some areas, I wasn't doing well at all. My addiction to self, evidenced in many ways, most regularly in the self-centered energy shaping the way I related, still had too much hold on me.

Perhaps I had closed the case too soon. Something was missing. Now in my mid-seventies, a question I had never before seriously explored came to mind: *What is the exact center of Christianity's good news?*

THE EXACT CENTER

I began to envision an unimaginable possibility that the three divine Persons had made available to me. Bear with me for a few pages. This possibility is just now forming in my mind. It may seem too esoteric, too exotic, too mysteriously other-worldly for us to realistically and practically lay hold of. We have bills to pay, doctors to see, relationships to heal and nurture, trash to take to the street on Fridays, and there are good days and bad days that we all experience. Can what I'm about to suggest that lies in the center of God's mind and heart as His story unfolds make a real difference in how I live in my smaller story? Yes, but *only if Christianity's good news is precisely what my thirsty soul most longs to both hear and experience!* The problem, of course, is that so many of us Christians are in touch only with lesser thirsts.

If we ask the Spirit to search our hearts and if we stay open to becoming aware of an ache in our soul, the ache of a deep, difficult to articulate unsatisfied longing, we may get in touch with a profoundly human desire that delights in the center of what the Gospel provides.

The exact center? In two sentences, my answer is this:

> *The Son enjoys a relationship with the Father that, as a bearer of God's image, I was created to similarly enjoy. Could it be that the love-generating joy of the Son poured into Him by the Father is now available to me, and the opportunity to know that joy is the center of the good news Jesus came to deliver?*
>
> *In different words: Thanks to the Father's plan for my*

> life, thanks to the Son's obedience to the Father that took Him to the cross, and thanks to the Spirit's ongoing work in me to turn my inward affection outward, away from me and toward God, I am now included in their community. I can now experience a taste of what Jesus knows in His relationship with the Father. I am now a son of God, small s, not God the Son, capital S; I'm still a created human, but alive as God's well-loved son.

―

Too mystical for you? At first glance it was for me. But shouldn't we expect that someone as incomprehensible as a three Person God might come up with a plan that mere humans living in a smaller story might have trouble understanding? The admittedly mystical prospect of literally entering into the relationship Jesus has with His Father brings the point of this book into focus. Let me explain.

Until the Second Coming, we know that our fellowship with Jesus in His relationship with the Father will remain soiled. Our self-centered nature is still addicting us, or at least trying to addict us, with the world's and the devil's help, to whatever relief and pleasure we can arrange for on our own. And when it becomes apparent, as it surely will, that God is not committed to the good life we naturally want, a life with maximum blessing and minimum trials, our old nature kicks into high gear.

We sense an opportunity seductively dangling before us, actually in us, in our thoughts and affections, an opportunity to feel relief from stress and to experience strong if temporary pleasure. In those moments of dangled opportunity, indulging an addictive self-serving urge, whether behavioral (looking at porn) or relational (using another for our satisfaction) seems attractively good, with little opposition from our better nature. Why so little opposition? Perhaps it hasn't been well fed. As a result, we won't see that we're being tempted into the enjoyment of evil.

If we're to fight the good fight, a fight that includes not only a battle against our addiction to self but also a fight to bring God's relational kingdom of holy love into our smaller story by how we relate, we will need to become aware of and steadily pursue a vision, a vision of the kind of man or woman we can become.

Visionary thinking requires answers to three questions. Who can I become? Who do I most want to become? And as I move toward that envisioned possibility, can I really expect to sense an awareness of a deep thirst in my soul that above all else longs to experience the Father's love for the Son coming alive in me, an experience that will reach fruition at the Second Coming?

Ponder those three questions long enough and deeply enough, guided by the Christian truth you already believe, and a passion to see Jesus face to face will often, not always, rise up in you as it sometimes rises up in me. I'll want to be personally with the One whose enjoyment of the Father's love He longs to fully share with me. To say I'll then be overwhelmed by the joyful worship that will flow out of me would be an understatement. It is then we earnestly long for the Lord's return when we will, for the first and eternal time, fully share in the joy of the love relationship between the Son and the Father. Our self-centered nature will then disappear into non-existence like the ghost it always was.

A friend recently sent me a quote he found in the writings of Pope Benedict XVI. His words awakened my desire for tastes of what is now available in my relationship with the Trinity, tastes that stir my appetite for what is fully available at the Second Coming.

> *"Eternal life is like plunging into the ocean of infinite life, the moment in which time – the before and after – no longer exists. We can only attempt to grasp the idea that such a moment is life in the fullest sense, a plunging ever anew into the vastness of being, in which we are simply overwhelmed with joy."*[2]

Still too mystical, even more so? The Pope was right. We can only attempt to grasp the idea that such a moment is life in the full sense. But we bear God's image, as relational beings, and we were created with a thirst for what will forever stagger our little minds and leave us overwhelmed with hope.

There is a path to follow that will help us attempt to grasp the opportunity that lies in the exact center of the Gospel: the opportunity to thirst for and in measure enter into the delights of the Father Son relationship. To put it mildly, they really do love each other. And we're to relate like them, to put the divine relationship of love on display with each other to the degree we enter into the reality of that relationship.

The path into the center will come into view when we see a vision of the "other things" I've mentioned, of what it would mean for us to dip our toes into the ocean of divine life even as we still live in this imperfect world as imperfect people.

As we move toward seeing that vision in the next chapter, keep in mind a wonderful truth: *as Christians we're already thirsty to become the men and women described by the vision.* We will, of course, fall short. But rather than feeling condemned, worthy only of God's wrath, we will more acutely thirst for the day when we will fall short no more. **We will then wait for the Second Coming with a passion fervent enough to compete with our addictive demand to feel good on our terms.**

We *can* live in the reality of the central message of Christianity. Hope is warranted. To activate that hope we need a vision of what it means to be a true disciple of Jesus, a disciple who longs to enter into the beauty of trinitarian life.

CHAPTER ELEVEN

The Power of a Much Needed Vision

Everyday I wish I were actively, eagerly, and with enduring patience waiting for the Lord's return. I want all my hope for the satisfaction of my soul's deepest thirst to be, as Peter expressed it, "in the gracious salvation that will" come to me "when Jesus Christ is revealed to the world" (I Peter 1: 13 NLT)[1].

Too often, my passionate hope lies elsewhere, from coffee served quickly at breakfast to good news from a biopsy report. I live most aware of my lesser thirsts. Why is that?

I do long for intense ardor to engulf me, a quiet but strong passion to meet Jesus face to face, a passion more alive than for anything less. I believe that such passion would further free me to accept whatever frustration or anguish I feel without demanding relief or pleasure, especially from illegitimate sources. I could then more resolutely resist addictive urges that still have their persuasive appeal, even after six decades of knowing Jesus.

Here's the problem. If I focus my efforts on ginning up enthusiasm for Christ's return, I'll live in daily defeat. Even praying for such enthusiasm seems futile. It must come from another direction.

My focus therefore has shifted. I'm more fervently asking God's Spirit to do whatever needs doing to make me the man I was saved to become, a living imitation of Jesus. With that shift in place, I'm drawn to the center of Gospel hope for today, to share in the life of the Trinity, more specifically to **fellowship with Jesus in His enjoyment of the Father's love.**

With that hope in mind, a vision is emerging, a vision of what might be developing in me as the Spirit does His work. What if, in always increasing measure:

- I hated sin more than I hated pain? What if I were convinced that suffering, physical, emotional, or spiritual, could arouse a thirst to share in the suffering of Jesus and thereby draw me closer to Him? What if I realized that whatever sin I enjoy is really the enjoyment of evil, a God-denying enjoyment that moves me further away from sharing in Christ's joy?
- I purposefully lived for what only God promised to do in me, for me, and through me? What if, like Moses, I deliberately turned away from whatever soul-deadening satisfaction this world can provide?
- I valued relational holiness, loving like Jesus, more than relational comfort, the shallow intimacy I too gladly welcome when others gratefully appreciate how good I am to them (at some sacrifice I might mention) and in response are good to me?
- I longed for soul-invigorating joy, the fruit of God's Spirit, more than I craved soul-numbing delights, the fruit of my flesh, rancid fruit that too often tastes good to me?

- I loved Jesus more than I loved anyone else (which Jesus told me to do): parents, spouse, children, friends, knowing He is the only source of the real life I most desire? What if (again as Jesus instructed) I properly "hated" all others as an alternate source of life, refusing to look to them for deep satisfaction when God seems distant? And what if I could then meaningfully love family and friends demanding nothing from them to earn my love?

The prospect of each of these virtues developing in my life draws me. It's the vision the Spirit is pursuing in me, a work He has already begun but has some distance yet to go. But He'll stay with it "until it is finally finished on the day when Christ Jesus returns" (Philippians 1: 6 NLT)[2].

I would argue that the five-element vision I've just described captures at least some of the vision which every Christian is most longing to see developed in their lives. Part of our deepest thirst during our time before Jesus comes is to become men and women marked by that level of maturity. Through Ezekiel, God promised to give us a "new heart" and to "put a new spirit" in us to remove our "strong, stubborn heart" from being the most powerful force within us, and to supply "a tender, responsive heart" that longs to share in the trinitarian life of love (Ezekiel 36: 27 NLT)[3]. Those truths from Ezekiel assure me that somewhere lodged deep in my soul I am more eager to live toward this vision of Christ-likeness than toward a managed vision of providing relief and pleasure for myself when I'm troubled or feel empty and inadequate.

Let me say it again. It's incredibly good news. **In the middle of our groaning and failure, we Christians are preeminently and insatiably thirsty, not for relief when struggling nor for temporarily satisfying pleasure when empty, but for what the Spirit makes possible**

when we embrace the vision of sharing the joy of Jesus as He lives in fellowship with the Father. We're thirsty to:
- hate sin more than pain;
- live for what only God gives, not for what the world gives;
- value the opportunity to give love more than to receive it, resting content in the truth that we're already loved with the love the Father has for His Son;
- feel the inexplicable joy we experience when we live thirsty for God, for soul-invigorating joy, not for the soul-deadening pleasure available in sin.
- love Jesus to a degree that we resist "loving" others with a sense of entitlement to a corresponding response from them.

—

A twisted version of Christianity, corrupted to its core, tells us we're more thirsty for the blessings of life, and that God is committed to providing them: good families, good friendships, good health, and of course, good money. The message resonates with believers who have yet to identify the center of Christianity, the relationship the Son enjoys with His Father which the Spirit invites us to share. This false message excites Christians who are aware of no greater thirst than for such blessings. Enjoy those blessings, but be aware that you're thirsty for so much more.

Fail to identify that greater thirst and a blessed life is then more valued than a forgiven life, a life worthy of judgment that is now lavished with love. A healed life is more touted than a called life, a life called to glorify God in times of blessings and hardships.

We must turn away from Exciting Christianity, a version that appeals to and legitimizes a priority desire to feel now what we will feel only in heaven. A pseudo-Christian life is offered, a life that never needs to be plagued by the exhaustion of unsatisfied desire, at least not in church. And daily repentance is not required, thanks to a shallow view of sin.

We must turn away from worship music lacking in sober lament, from music that only generates an emotional high that convinces would-be worshippers that they are worshipping. But let's not turn away from rich praise and the joy that it brings.

We must turn away from theatrical preaching that, perhaps unwittingly, tells people "whatever their itching ears want to hear"; preaching that ups the danger of leading professing Christians to "reject the truth and chase after myths" (2 Timothy 4: 3 NLT)[4]. Such preaching leaves listeners living in the illusion of spiritual maturity, an illusion sustained by occasional tweaks and re-charged inspiration Sunday after Sunday.

We must turn away too from ministry efforts and missional endeavors that centrally focus on changing others' lives for the better, on ridding culture of racism and corporate greed, and on making the world a safer place to live. Worthy goals all, but prioritize them and Christians will be distracted from the true priority of becoming relationally mature beyond the above efforts.

The more Christians prioritize Christ's central command to love as He loves, the more the church will compassionately and actively oppose such social wrongs as racism, world hunger, and homelessness. Organizations that exist to correct such wrongs should be welcomed and supported by Christians, yet always with a principal concern that we have a Christ-like heart to relationally love others well even as we express an active burden to see social wrongs righted.

If we're to discover our deepest thirst for what is offered from the center of Christianity, we must turn toward biblical Christianity that moves us in at least three directions:

toward prayer, asking the Spirit to expose our controlling thirst for less than what Christianity centrally offers, and to arouse our thirst for what the human soul most wants;

toward Scripture, affirming the Bible to be the actual Word of God that we must hear. As Brennan Manning once wrote: "If God is speaking, the best thing we can do is listen"[5], knowing that in Scripture God speaks with final authority;

toward relationality, toward a Christianity that calls Christians to pay careful attention to one another, to what is going on in us that we too often hide, with the purpose, not of judging, gossiping, or criticizing, but of stirring one another to love well and do good (see Hebrews 10: 24)[6].

Well, where does all this leave us? I've written ten chapters, and am now about to complete Chapter Eleven, driven by an awareness that I'm addicted, addicted to my immediate self-interest in whatever form that may take. I don't, however, call myself an addict. Doing so would establish an incorrect identity. I'm a *Christian* still struggling with addictive self-interest, but fully loved by God.

I want to understand and experience the freedom that is mine in Christ, not only the freedom from condemnation but from the controlling power of sin. I'm not sure why, but as I developed fresh interest in the Gospel's freedom, something caught my attention: *it has been years since either I preached on the Second Coming or I heard someone else make it the central topic of a sermon.*

That observation led me, I believe prodded by the Spirit, to wonder if passionately waiting for Christ's return would somehow free me to demand nothing now as I live in this world and to expect everything I was created and re-created to enjoy in the next world. Could truly eager waiting for then provide the motivation and will power I need now to better resist addictive urges?

In severe contradiction to my secular psychological training, I identified those urges as the voice of my evil self-centered nature that persuasively suggested I assume responsibility to provide for my own relief from stress in any way that seemed to work and to arrange for whatever sort of pleasure takes away the sting of loneliness, fear, failure, and any other disturbing emotion or condition.

I wanted to explore how my holy other-centered nature could release whatever was needed to counter the pull of my evil self-centered nature and help me reliably say no to addictive desires. That exploration became this book.

So now it is mostly written. Most of my thoughts on the matter have been shared, explained, and defended as best I could.

But a few final chapters seem in order, to tidy loose ends up a bit, and with raw honesty to share how successful I've been, or not, in enjoying a new passion for Christ's return that is providing a new freedom in my battle against addiction. Perhaps I should also say something about how well I am tracking with the Spirit in reaching that five-element vision of maturity.

I suppose what I'm about to write will either encourage or discourage you, either inspire you to re-read my words and suggest others read them or throw the book in the nearest trash can.

I hope in both cases it will have the former effect, but I don't want to dissemble; I don't want to write words designed to compromise what I understand to be biblical truth or to disingenuously present palatable ideas for the purpose of being well received. I must let the chips of authenticity fall where they may.

Part III

POWERFUL WAITING

A Pathway to Freedom

CHAPTER TWELVE

The Pathway Revealed

Is any book ever finished? I've written nearly thirty of them, and in each case I've turned in the manuscript to my publisher with a nagging sense that more needed to be said.

This book is no different. Three more chapters, which I expect to be the last, will leave much unsaid. I do, however, believe that what I now plan to write will add significant value to what I've already written in eleven chapters.

One value might be clarification of a few ideas I may have insufficiently made clear. If I can forestall misunderstanding, I'd like to do so. Plus, a healthy dose of realism is in order before I wrap things up. Whatever insights I've picked up, hopefully from the Spirit, have not yet touched my struggles deeply enough to keep me from too often falling off the narrow road.

Little is more disconcerting to me than reading authors presenting really important truths without providing a path to the enjoyment of those truths in the rough and tumble of life. Forgive my cynicism. I do sometimes wonder if great thinkers harnessed to the Bible who write well understand how distant and uninvolved God can seem during hard days. Their words first excite then frustrate me. I'm left having no idea what to do with the marvelous truths they have clearly communicated. One excellent writer I've been reading made a strong point in telling me the Holy Spirit is the one who unites me with the life of Christ. What would it mean for me to *cooperate* with His work, which is more than *believing* in His work? He never said.

But I am neither proud enough, smart enough, or insightful enough to think I will ever give the final word on any subject of real importance, certainly not on the subject of a possible connection between eagerly waiting for the Second Coming and achieving a Spirit-granted satisfying measure of self control over our addiction to ourselves. But perhaps I can offer a little clarity.

ANOTHER LOOK AT ADDICTIVE BEHAVIORS

By the way, in earlier chapters I tried to make clear that when I speak of addictive disorders, all of which draw power from our inveterate self-centeredness, I'm thinking of more than addictions to such things as alcohol, drugs, sex, food, and money. I think of them as *acquisition addictions* where people make choices, often very bad ones, to acquire and use whatever helps them feel good.

Alcohol and drugs dull pain and lift spirits, quickly. Sex functions similarly. Whether in marriage or outside, a demand for sexual pleasure qualifies as an addiction. So too does a seemingly uncontrollable demand for sexual pleasure from sources the Bible insists are perverted. In a different category of addiction, watch someone wolf down a ketchup smothered cheeseburger with a generous side of crispy onion rings, then if you observe the performance repeated a day later, you have reason to suspect you're seeing an acquisition disorder in progress. Earning money through hard work is, of course, legitimate and, depending on the nature of the work, honorable. But there is a thin line between grateful satisfaction for abundant financial resources and an entitled expectation for the abundance to continue or bloat. Most would agree that each of the above can rightly be seen as an addiction, an *acquisition addiction*. But there is such a thing as *relational addictions*. They are many, perhaps more subtle and rarely thought of as addictions, but they always harm relationships and should be seen as a significant problem that has led to relational poverty for many. Let me offer one of a hundred possible examples: covetousness. Most of us covet something from others. When we greedily desire recognition and approval from others as if our soul health depended on it, we are relationally addicted. From all walks of life, there are many who yearn to be included in an inner ring, whether in family relationships, relationships at work, or relationships in church.

A lustful eagerness to feel wanted or valued by another reliably dictates how one engages in social conversations, marital exchanges, parental responses to children, job related interactions, sometimes even dialogue between a therapist and a client. The result is relational poverty.

But most relational addictions remain unrecognized, unchallenged, and unchanged. They seem to the one addicted as natural and unnoticed as breathing.

Suppose we find the humble convicting courage to admit we are controlled by one or more of these addictive urges. Suppose, too, we truly hate the addiction even though we "love" the pleasure provided when we indulge the urge. As Christians, suppose we sincerely long to live free of addictive control, wanting to freely receive and give divine love, to live in glad obedience to our Lord, and to keep in step with the Spirit's promptings. What then? What are we to do?

Psychology has come up with a variety of treatment protocols for addictive disorders. Liberal religion offers its own methods to help, which in some cases might mean to encourage indulgence as a legitimate and normal path to emotional well-being. Evangelical churches develop programs that claim to blend the best of well researched psychology with conservative theology, programs designed to assist members who present themselves as addicts to overcome their addiction.

What drives me is simple. I can't get past the assumption that the Gospel of Christ, the good news that locates its center in the love between the Father and the Son which the Spirit arranges for us to enjoy, provides a unique path to be less controlled by self-centered inclinations and more strongly drawn to a life of holy love with the Trinity, and to divine love shared with others. One example: a soul filled with divine love will be quick to recognize the relational demand to impress another.

IS THERE MORE TO THE PATH TO FREEDOM?

As G.K. Chesterton once remarked, "the secret business of heaven is joy". The secret is no longer hidden. Salvation is centered in sharing the joy the Son experiences in His relationship with the Father. That joy, I submit, will powerfully compete with the self-serving and self-managed pleasure that addictions provide. And note this: addictive pleasure blights our experience of divine joy.

But there is a gap between believing such high-level truth and living in it. Can such lofty truth be brought down into our everyday lives and do something about our struggle with addictions that nothing else can do?

Paul thought so. He wrote a short letter to a fellow worker named Titus who Paul was asking to follow up on the missionary labors he had already brought to the island of Crete. The islanders on Crete were widely known to be debauched, stubborn, hard to get along with sinful people. Paul wanted Titus to know that people addicted to evil in its worst forms could be transformed by the power of the Gospel. He therefore wrote these words to Titus:

"For the grace of God has been revealed, bringing salvation to all people. And we are instructed to turn from godless living and sinful pleasures. We should live in this evil world with wisdom, righteousness, and devotion to God, while we look forward with hope to that wonderful day when the glory of our great God and Savior, Jesus Christ, will be revealed. He gave his life to free us from every kind of sin, to cleanse us, and to make us his very own people, totally committed to doing good deeds" (Titus 2: 11-12 NLT)[1].

I draw encouragement from those words. Maybe I'm on the right track. As I've been writing this book, my burden from the beginning has been to explore the impact of Gospel truth, especially the trinitarian life Christians share, on our battle against addictions. With both Paul and Peter (remember Peter told us to put all our hope on the return of Jesus), I am persuaded that living in the sure hope of the Second Coming has something invigorating to do with you and I turning away from godless living and sinful pleasures. I believe that actively pursing a vision of spiritual formation as we live now in this evil world will somehow free us to resist addictive urges. I further believe that sharing in the love relationship between the Father and the Son will strengthen us against the appeal of evil behaving and relating as nothing else can do.

Have you just sensed a "but" is coming? It is. *But* I fear that I may have given you the impression that waiting eagerly for the Second

Coming, *plus* pursuing the vision of spiritual formation, *plus* recognizing what lies in the center of Christianity and trusting the Spirit for us to live there, *plus* regular involvement in self-examining and Gospel celebrating prayer, in thoughtful study of the Bible coupled with meditation on its truth, and in authentic community where people are open and grace is given, would provide everything we need to resist compelling sinful desires. If that's what you heard from me in the first eleven chapters, I've miscommunicated. Let me clarify.

I do *not* believe that eagerly waiting for the Lord's return is sufficient for us to resist temptation. It's necessary but not sufficient. *Something more* is required.

I do *not* believe that a diligent pursuit of spiritual disciplines designed to form us like Jesus will provide the self control we need to say a firm no to sinful urges, unless accompanied by *something more*.

I do *not* believe that the promise of joy for believers who join the Son in the shared delights of the Father's love will by itself empower us to keep addictive cravings under control. We need *something more*.

I do *not* believe that self-examining worshipful prayer, probing Bible study, and relationships within authentic community will change addicts into former addicts. *Something more,* not less, is essential.

What is it?

CHAPTER THIRTEEN

Something More: The Power of Choice

As I struggle to understand what can be done to help Christians live holy lives, specifically to fight against surrendering to unholy desires, I have a rather lofty goal in mind. For myself and others, I want to go beyond gaining control over our addictions. The goal I'm after is one that most approaches to treating addictions cannot deliver.

Without tapping into resources available in Christianity or with depending instead on guidelines laid down by liberal Christianity, treatments sometimes do in fact produce results.

Alcoholics stop drinking.

Drug addicts live free of further abuse.

Anorexics eat normal portions of healthy food.

Cutters stop cutting.

Even relational addicts, for example men who pride themselves on stoic personas or displays of intelligence, women who relate either subserviently or overbearingly, perhaps through counseling learn to relate in ways that foster healthy relationships.

I would never denigrate such laudable improvements. Nor would I deny the value of exploring inner dynamics in understanding and getting a handle on addictive patterns. More on that later.

But I'm chasing after more. Of course I want to see addictive behaviors resisted, even reversed into commendable self-discipline. But the Gospel aims higher. Christianity makes it possible for anyone no matter their addictive struggles not only to gain strong control over their unique temptations but also to relate with divine love flowing out of their Spirit-created other centered nature into others. Perhaps a Christian way to help addicts will also release them to be lovers.

I've taken great pains already to suggest what is included in a Christian way to move toward these worthy goals. For the impossible to become possible, it is necessary to focus expectantly on the Lord's return; to intentionally pursue spiritual formation; to learn what it means to live as a son or daughter of God who enjoys the Father's love in similar measure to the Son of God, always the eternal Son, who delights in that love more than He delights in anything else; to engage in self-examining prayer, in thoughtful time in the Bible, and in relationships with others who live in authentic community.

But something more is required. If we're to turn away from evil tendencies and turn toward godly relating, *we must recover the power of choice, the freedom to reject wrong choices and to make good choices.*

No, I'm by no means suggesting we simply, perhaps forcefully, instruct porn addicts to stop watching porn, to merely exhort anorexics to eat more, or to admonish folks struggling with same-sex attraction to feel romantic toward the opposite sex. We might as well tell short people to grow taller or tall folks to shrink a little. No one can make that choice. And telling people addicted to self-centeredness, which we all are at a profound level, to stop making self-centered choices and instead choose to make other-centered choices doesn't help much. Legalism isn't the answer. The best it can hope for is conformity to a standard, an appearance of other-centeredness still rooted in self-concerned energy.

But what about biblical injunctions? Doesn't Scripture command that certain choices be made and others resisted? A few examples drawn from many: don't shift from the hope of the Gospel even when evil seems to be winning (see Colossians 1:22)[1]; don't give into ungodly living or sinful desires even when doing so feels inevitable (see Titus 2:12)[2] see to it that you love one another as Jesus loves you (see John 15:12)[3]. So many bad choices we're told to not make and so many good choices we're instructed to make. Obedience isn't always our strong suit.

We know what it means to give into a sinful urge without experiencing the giving in as a choice. And when we try to make the good choice to not give in, too often we feel powerless. It seems we can't. Still, God tells us to make good choices, and holds us accountable to do so, dating us far back as Genesis 2:17[4]: "...of the tree of the knowledge of good and evil, you shall not eat". Then again in Joshua 29:15[5]: "choose this day whom you will serve". *Somehow, we are to recover the freedom to choose and the power of choice.* But how? My assumption? Through the Gospel.

—

RECLAIMING THE FREEDOM TO CHOOSE

Begin with this: the freedom God gave us centers in the ability to choose. Programmed robots cannot bring glory to a relational God.

But when we became sinners, we lost the freedom to do right, as God defines right. Doing wrong became such an effortless choice it didn't feel like a choice, any more than breathing feels like a choice. And yet if I am to gain even a measure of control over addictive urges, at least in the beginning stages and perhaps until I die, a choice is required. In order to love another with the sacrificial suffering love of Jesus, though a mature Christian will desire to offer that kind of love, a choice will need to be made. Let me say it again: **somehow, we must experience the power of choice and thus to recover the freedom to choose.**

I am suggesting that the choice to deny sin its power to control what we do and to relate to others with the life-giving love of the Trinity is a choice that can be made only if the choice is **well informed** and **meaningfully influenced.**

The idea is really quite simple.

INFORMED CHOICE

A choice to resist an evil urge and move instead toward holy relating must first be persuasively informed by at least two core truths: One, *only Christianity and the Christ of Christianity can lead us into the life the human soul was designed to live, and can therefore most enjoy.*

The chooser will best be persuaded of the truthfulness of that truth if it is presented by someone whose evident contentment and style of relating is unmistakably genuine by virtue of their relationship with Christ. By example, such a person draws others to Christ by illustrating that only the truth of the Gospel can satisfy a human soul as much as it can be satisfied while still living in this evil world as a not yet glorified person.

There are times when God uses difficult news to shine a convicting spotlight on someone's ongoing addictive behavior. In the strange ways of the Spirit, the wickedness of yielding to sinful urges then becomes painfully apparent. It is then a Christian is bothered enough by his or her failure to be meaningfully open to the Spirit's further work, enabling the Christian to be deeply drawn to the truth stated above.

Two, *only the three Person God is telling a soul-satisfying story that will reach its forever satisfying consummation when for a second time, God will look at all He created and declare "It is good! It's very good!"* Those same words were heard the first time shortly after creation, before sin and trouble began. It will not be heard again until the Second Coming. That realization whets our appetite for that day. So, we wait eagerly, anticipating shalom, learning to demand nothing now and expecting everything then.

Paul told us to "think about these things", beautiful, honorable, commendable, pure truth (see Philippians 4:8)[6]. Discover these truths in Scripture. Study the Christian books that unpack them. Read the stories of men and women who lived them. And consider our desperate straits if none of these things are true.

Then listen again to Paul writing to young Timothy: you must "continue in what you have learned and have firmly believed, knowing from whom you learned it" (2 Timothy 3:14 ESV)[7]. Only by long continuing in God's truth will it gain the power to inform our choices.

We must also, however, reckon with disturbing truth: when we yield to sinful urges, whether behavioral or relational, we are in that moment living in the enjoyment of evil; a repugnant thought. The enjoyment of evil can seem to more fully satisfy an empty soul than the living truth of the Gospel. We therefore need to often remind ourselves that evil's pleasures (1) are short-lived; (2) harm our souls, driving us away from abiding in Christ and therefore, until we repent, leaving us incapable of enjoying or sharing God's love; and (3) are worthy of the devil's children, not God's.

I conclude that a choice informed is a choice we can make. Truth sets us free. Jesus said so (see John 8: 32)[8]. But a choice set free by truth will still bump up against sin's captivating appeal. Our truth-informed choice needs additional force.

INFLUENCED CHOICE

I've often puzzled over what it means to depend on the Holy Spirit to do what I should. In younger years and still today, I hear that I must live in the Spirit's strength and not my own. Does that mean I'm only a dead leaf lying still on the ground unable to move until the wind blows? I think not. Paul tells us to work out our own continuing rescue from sin, knowing "it is God who works in you, both to will and to work for his good pleasure" (Philippians 2:13 ESV)[9]. Apparently, I have a real part in the Spirit's work. Somehow, He influences my will so that I make choices that please God.

An informed choice is a choice we realize we *can* make, knowing it lines up nicely with truth that grips us deeply. But in order for an informed choice to become a choice we *will* make, it must also become an influenced choice, influenced by deep human thirst. It is here the Gospel, and only the Gospel, makes a critical difference in our understanding of what it will take to resist sinful urges. Here's how:

> *Because of regeneration, of being made alive to God, alive in Christ, and alive with the Holy Spirit, the most compelling thirst in the soul of a Christian is a thirst for holiness, to know the God of love and to live to make Him known.*

The arousal of that thirst is a work of the Holy Spirit; the choice to stop digging leaky wells and move toward the well of living water is our work. But in our day of unchallenged comfortable Christianity, it is easy to hear that we want God more than anyone or anything less, nod our heads in smiling agreement, then pick up a shovel and dig another leaky well. Until we experience an unmatched thirst for God, we will move on with our lives, living for lesser thirsts we're more eager to slake.

I fear many books flooding the Christian market, books met with enthusiasm, encourage Christians to settle for comfortable Christianity, believing it is God's good news that, with prayer, life will work much as we want it to work. We then live to satisfy lesser thirsts.

One book clearly warns us of that danger. In *Religious Affections*[10], a classic by Jonathan Edwards, we're told that all of us gravitate toward whatever attracts us the most. A thirst for ginger ale will not be satisfied with water. So we open a can of Canada Dry. A thirst for wine will not lead us to open the can of ginger ale, but rather to uncork a bottle of Merlot.

I must ask myself: in any given moment, whenever is now, am I most drawn to Christianity, most thirsty for what only the God of Christianity offers, or do I experience a stronger desire for something less? If so, I am vulnerable to justifying a bad choice because it feels really good. We then are living with a wrong understanding of morality: *those people are moral who live true to whatever is naturally felt to be their deepest thirst.*

By that standard, Hugh Hefner was a highly moral man. He lived to pursue satisfaction of what he experienced to be his strongest desire, sexual pleasure. He was aware, I presume, of no greater thirst.

Adolph Hitler, too, would be classified as moral by a wrong understanding of morality. His choices in life indicated he was most attracted to self-exalting power that let him freely express his unfounded animus against an entire race. If a thirst to be a good person according to God's standard ever crept into his consciousness, he suppressed it. Neither Hitler nor Hefner, two extreme examples to make an important point obvious, made choices influenced by a thirst to be forgiven by God, embraced by God, and to put Jesus on display by how they related to others.

But let's be clear: no one will be excused for rejecting the Gospel on the grounds that they felt no attraction to it. Listen to Paul. He tells us that God's holy wrath is directed toward those who "suppress the truth" about God, truth that "is plain to them because God has showed it to them". Even His "eternal power and divine nature" are evident in "things that have been made" (Romans 1:18-20 ESV)[11]. No one's plea to be excused for their sin will be accepted. Everyone's plea for undeserved forgiveness will.

A longing lives, perhaps unanswered, in every Christian's soul, a longing for God, to know and glorify Him, a longing that is stronger than any other. And yet along with others I reflexively find ways to dull that thirst, to be directed by lesser thirsts whose satisfaction I may be able to manage, to gain satisfaction on demand, under my control. I sometimes pray to God wanting nothing more from Him than more money, improved health, and relational happiness with family and friends.

Should He not come through, should financial worries continue, further surgery be needed, or disturbing tensions remain in a close relationship, a thirst for relief from struggles and for pleasure that numbs painful emotions feels pressing. Familiar ways to satisfy that thirst tempt me, ways I know I should resist.

We will desire to make sin-rejecting choices and life-giving choices only when we become aware of our most significant holy thirst.

It is in the hands of the Spirit that some form of suffering—disappointment, rejection, a bad health diagnosis, whatever it might be—brings our deepest thirst to awareness. When troubles come, we are to treat them as an opportunity for something good to develop in our mind and heart (see James 1:2-4)[12]. Two clear options present themselves: run from God in angry despair, wailing on your bed because God is not protecting you as you wish; or tremble and trust, lament over fallenness in yourself, others and the world, but trust Him to bring you into the Son's enjoyment of the Father's love, crying from your heart for exactly that, knowing it is to that He is unalterably committed (see Hosea 7:14)[13].

Then with the psalmist we will learn to say "… for me it is good to be near God" (Psalm 73:28 ESV)[14], and with another to sing "As a deer pants for flowing streams, so pants my soul for you, O God. My soul thirsts for God, for the living God" (Psalm 42:1 ESV)[15]. We feel our thirst for God. Our choices are now influenced by holy thirst, thirst that attracts us to God.

All that I've written in this chapter adds up to this:

*A choice informed by God's truth is a choice we **can** make: IT IS POSSIBLE*

*A choice influenced by our thirst for God is a choice we **will** make: IT IS DESIRED*

An informed choice and an influenced choice, coupled with all we've already discussed, is the something more we need to better resist addictive urges and to release divine life out of us into others. And it is that release of real life into others that deepens a thirst which no addiction will quench.

CHAPTER FOURTEEN

Wrapping Up: From My Heart to Yours

I've been lying on the couch looking away from my writing desk, hoping to find the energy needed to begin this final chapter, sensing it might be the most important of the chapters that make up this book. Maybe not, but maybe. I initially laid down to relax a back sore from sitting on my desk chair for six hours, re-writing my fifth and final draft of Chapter Thirteen.

When I flopped on the couch I hadn't planned to pray, but I soon found myself talking with God, my heavenly Father, in many ways like my earthly father, a man full of grace. Several sentences flowed into my mind, brought there no doubt by some of what I wrote in earlier chapters, which I had just re-read before resting my back. The sentences expressed thoughts that seemed strangely alive with desire and hope. As best I now remember, the following sentences were the ones running through my mind that God listened to:

> *"Father, I know I'm Your son by grace. You made that clear in the Bible. But I can scarcely imagine what it would mean for me to personally, to actually experience and really feel, the same love for me that You have for Jesus, Your Son by nature. He never disappointed You. I do, all too often. Your love for Him kept Him moving through 33 years of life all the way to the cross.*
>
> *My small soul must be having a hard time experiencing, really knowing in the Hebrew sense, the large love You have for me. I still give in to addictive urges. But I believe You do love me. I've felt it, sometimes intensely, even abidingly for seasons. But I want to experience Your love for me so much more fully, so fully that there is nothing I want more, so fully that I value nothing more, so fully that I enjoy nothing more, so fully that I would be willing to do anything that would display my love to You, and Your love to others.*
>
> *I'm not there, but I think I'm on the road. My thirst is real. And what I've written in this book has drawn me along a little further."*

As I read my thirst-filled words, I'm more convinced that to whatever degree I experience God's love as His son by grace, to that degree I will both resist evil urges, (assuming I recognize them as evil) and love others a bit more like Jesus loves, giving them a small taste of divine love. When I finished that prayer, I wanted to get up from my couch and write.

Well, I just wanted to share that. Now I have two more things to say before I put my pen down. Yes, I do all my writing with a pen and pad of paper. First, a personal word to you, a reader who has stayed with me till now. Second, a personal word about me, about what, if anything, these previous thirteen chapters have done and are doing for me what I pray they could do for you. I'm wary. My pen is on the paper. Time to write.

A Personal Word to You

You struggle with addiction. Of course you do. Everyone does. Maybe not the obvious ones that the word addiction calls easily to mind: addictions to alcohol, drugs, sex, food or money. Or maybe. Lots of folks, lots of Christians, struggle with these addictions without others knowing. But one thing I do know. Like me, you struggle with the addiction that's been part of you since the day you were conceived, an addiction to yourself, to your own best interests according to your wisdom.

And until you were saved by Jesus, you were naturally bent to serve your own interests by turning anywhere but to God. Now you're a Christian. But the addiction to yourself is still with you. You can't escape it. At times it seems that the satisfaction you long for can be found in a source that lies outside of God's good will for you. If nothing else, you sometimes relate with others intending to get more than you give. We all do. Really mature Christians more often relate to give more than to get, but never always, never with pure motives.

If you do drink too much or use illicit drugs, you have plenty of opportunities to indulge. There's a liquor store nearby. Grocery stores are probably closer. And pot for medicinal purposes, maybe for recreational use, is available, in some states legally in that store with symbols or words painted green. For more serious stuff, dealers can be found. A walk downtown might lead you to one, or perhaps even at a party with Christian friends.

If sex addiction is your battle, temptations exist everywhere: a computer screen, most movies, too many television shows. A visit to the mall, where you work, the school you attend, even church – they all provide occasions to lust, as does your fertile imagination.

Maybe food is your go-to, mostly sweets. Or money. Self-centeredness, the demand to feel good that at times feels necessary, maybe as your right, can land pretty much anywhere. Always in relationships if nowhere else. Get something from someone. Approval, maybe support for something you're doing for God. If that's a demand, you're addicted. Perhaps it's respect you want so you can feel significant. Curiosity from another will help you feel heard, less alone. Affection makes you feel desirable, wanted. It's legitimately human to want all the above, and more. It's illegitimate, sinful, to demand it, to believe it's your entitled right. It's not. But it is a normal healthy desire. Again like you, I've been exposed as self-centered, selfishly expecting approval, support for my godly calling, respect so I can feel important, curiosity about me that lets me feel someone is interested in my life, and affection so I will know I'm desirable.

I've been exposed by God. All the above is true of me, and I suspect of you. And yet it's from Him I receive everything I need to live the life I most want to live. It's good, a true blessing, when others approve, support, respect, offer curiosity and affection. Enjoy when it comes. Live for it, expect it as a right, demand it, and you're relationally addicted.

Satan is at his devilish best when he's directing our relational addictions. He's a liar. Without realizing what you're doing, you are manipulating someone, defensively retreating from someone, exacting revenge on someone. If an active conscience lets you know the evil you're enjoying, Satan will encourage you to think it's not all that wrong; or if it is wrong, it is still justified. Someone has hurt you, even a loving spouse, maybe a son or daughter, a friend, could be your pastor or priest or your parent or therapist. They had no right or reason to treat you as they did. Maybe still do. Welcome to Satan's world.

You've suffered. You are suffering, if not physically (when no one's giving you enough sympathy), then emotionally, from memories of hurt that you rehearse to the point where they seem like today's hurt. You have plenty of current disappointments to add to the bitter memories. If people knew your suffering, they would not judge you for however you've reacted. You'd be excused.

God knows your suffering, every moment of it, every pain lodged in your soul. He grieves with you. But He does not excuse your self-protective way of relating. Nor does He understand it as a reasonable reaction to suffering. He does something better. He forgives you!

You're a Christian. You've failed. You know it. You don't deny it. You own it and confess it for what it is, relational sin. You're looking out for your own interests, not so much for the interests of others. Maybe you've self-medicated with porn, or with one more drink. You're holding a grudge and it feels good to feel superior to the one who hurt you.

But now you realize you've failed, in God's eyes, by His standard of holy, merciful, compassionate, self-sacrificing love. Everyone does, in some form, every day. We fall short of the relational glory of God, the way He loves others at any cost to Himself. You see it. You know it. Perhaps privately, you've sunk into the prideful depths of self loathing.

Oh, I know. You're like me. You hide it well. Better to maintain a godly persona. Why risk someone's scorn or give reason for gossip? You're still good for a laugh; you still speak of God's goodness even while privately you're angry at Him.

At 2 in the morning when you can't sleep, you're wondering: am I a loser, a fake, a hopeless case? Is Christianity even true? Your Christianity, your God, isn't working the way you expected. Where is God? He seems to be elsewhere. Who am I? A Christian backslider? Maybe I'm not even saved. Now what?

I've been there. Still am at moments, more often at 4 in the morning, not 2. We're not that different. What did you expect? To some degree, we're still both addicted to ourselves, wanting God, others, and the world to give us what we want, what we need to be happy, to do things our way. They should! Then we would live godly lives and resist sinful urges. So we think.

Now what's my counsel? You might be drawn to it. You might not like it. It's working for me. Perfectly? Of course not. Meaningfully? Yes. I haven't given up. I'm thirsty for God, more than ever. Sometimes while driving my car singing old hymns, I cry for joy. I want God! He wants me! And sometimes, more than in earlier days, it's showing in the way I relate.

A brief caveat. Not only do I *not* have a five-step guaranteed plan in mind, but I also will *not* offer a set of suggestions that clearly illuminates a path that can be easily and strictly followed. But I do have some thoughts provoked by your intense longing and mine, maybe not yet discovered, to share so richly in the Father's love for His Son that addictions lose their seemingly irresistible power. And these thoughts meld into a series of suggestions to embrace and follow. A foolproof plan outlined by these suggestions? A guarantee of no more yielding to sinful urges? Hardly. But helpful ideas for walking the narrow road to life? Empowering suggestions? I think so. I'm living them, longing to live them better.

Here's my counsel. As I said, you may like it. You may not. Either way, here it is:

- **Be where you are!** Live in your darkness, your confusion, your struggle, your failure. It's your best chance for meeting God. He tends to meet us where we are, not where we pretend to be or wish we were. The degree to which you come clean and pretend about nothing is the degree to which you may discover your deepest thirst for God, who alone is guaranteed to still want you. You long to be wanted – at your worst.

- **Talk to someone else.** One person will do. Someone you believe to be an honest struggler, someone least likely to be defensive, superior, or judgmental. Pray for someone to be *with* you, not to help, sympathize, correct, or scold; certainly someone who you wouldn't expect to smile and recite platitudes or try to figure you out. When you're *with* someone, new thoughts come to mind; hope re-kindles. You will not feel so alone. And that experience will direct you to the only true source of feeling seen and wanted, not alone. Remember Jesus who said: "The hour is coming… when you will be gathered each to his own home, and will leave me alone. Yet I am not alone, for the Father is with me" (John 16:22 ESV)[1]. Therefore demand no one else to be perfectly with you. Let their best "withness" draw you into the withness Jesus felt with His Father.

- **Keep talking with God**, in conversational prayer. Own and express the ugly truth that you know what it means to enjoy evil. Don't back away from that heinous reality by thinking of someone who failed more visibly. But realize you're not alone in the depths of your sin. Remember what Paul said in Romans 7: 19: "For I do not do the good I want, but the evil I do not want is what I keep on doing"[2]. Then consider to what heights of holy living that confession brought him.

- **Keep talking.** You'll know when it's time to listen, when you're desperate to know how God is responding to all you've said. Time to read John 3:16[3], to read Romans 1-8[4], and so many other Scriptures that come to mind. Read John Stott, *The Cross of Christ*[5].
- **Let Gospel truth burn** deeply in a desperate, humbled soul. Only at your ugliest will you most clearly see God's beauty. You will not completely stop sinning. Repentance is required every day. But redemption, regeneration, and reconciliation – the wonder of grace makes it possible for the sinner and the saint you are to enjoy God's love and spread it around.

You're on your way. Confession, not shame, will be an ongoing part of your journey on the narrow road. Struggle as you must. Fail when you do. Repent quickly, celebrate grace, and keep on, resolute in your thirst to know the love of God more and more deeply. You're now living the Christian life.

CHAPTER FIFTEEN

All About Me? NO! All About Christ in Me, The Hope of Glory

I planned to finish this book with Chapter Fourteen. Now here I am writing Chapter Fifteen. Let me explain. I have never outlined a book before writing one, much to the chagrin of my publishers. I can't do it. I won't do it. It would mess with my rhythm. A thought occurs, I write a chapter. Only then does the next chapter come into focus. And so on until I call it a book.

When I began Chapter Fourteen, I had in mind to write two personal words to complete the book, one to you and one about me, sharing whatever impact I thought my writing was having on my life. The personal word to you, my reader, developed into more words than I anticipated, enough to make up a full chapter. So I shifted gears a bit, deciding to write a sort of addendum, a few paragraphs about my journey through addictive struggles as the book was unfolding, nothing more than one more page at the end of Chapter Fourteen.

That plan came unglued last night.

Yesterday was the second of three days of medically required isolation. Two days on steroids, prescribed after a physician planted radioactive seeds into a few malignant tumors in my liver, produced a common side effect: sleeplessness.

I crawled into our guestroom bed last night a little before ten. I dozed for maybe an hour, then woke up wired and laid under the covers thinking about the message of this book. Thought time lasted more than an hour. I got weary with thinking and picked up a good novel by Louise Penny already half read. The murder mystery was riveting, but a new wave of fatigue descended on me. I sagged, then managed to doze again, briefly. By 3am, I was wide awake. I returned to my thoughts. Many came. In my drugged condition, my mind flew in directions that felt enlivening, invigorating, and liberating. I wondered. Had my induced stupor brought on the excitement? When it wore off, would the fresh thoughts still seem fresh?

Morning came. Two cups of strong coffee cleared the fog. The thoughts remained, not only still alive but somewhat organized. I sensed their promise to lead me toward greater freedom from addictive urges. More than a few paragraphs are now in the works. Hence, Chapter Fifteen.

—

A Personal Word: Less About Me, More About Christ in Me, the Hope of Glory.

If not the most distinctively human gift God gave us, this one ranks near the top: *the freedom to choose.* With God-granted human dignity, what Pascal referred to as the dignity of causality, I am free to choose my direction through life. The gift is real. Adam and Eve made their choice. And now we too remain capable of making choices, regrettably the same one, always, at least early on.

We've uniformly followed in our first parents' footsteps, making a disastrously bad choice. We chase after sources that promise life but deliver death. Somehow we convince ourselves our choices are good, necessary, if not wise.

We've become addicted to bad choices, but we see ourselves as victims, not free choosers. "Why do you watch porn?" a wife asks her husband, "I'm sorry, honey. I can't help it. I'm addicted". Someone gets fed up with her friend. "You keep your distance from me, from everybody. Our friendship doesn't feel real." "But I've been hurt so badly. I've got to protect myself. I wish you would understand. I really have no choice. I have to play it safe."

Relational poverty is now widespread. Soul to soul connection is not the norm, it's rare. We get on with life by denying how alone we feel. Jesus came to give us relational life. But on our own, no one chooses to seize the opportunity for the joy He provides. We prefer to manage our lives, looking out for our own felt well-being.

I have that on good authority. Listen to Paul: "no one seeks for God. All have turned aside…" (Romans 3:11, 12 ESV)[1]. He was quoting a much earlier writer, a psalmist who recognized the same tragedy. "The Lord looks down from heaven on the children of man, to see if there are any who understand" – who live wisely – "who seek after God. They have all turned aside, together they have become corrupt; there is no one who does good" – who chooses wisely – "not even one" (Psalm 14:2 ESV)[2].

A severe indictment, one our culture denies: "there's always a few bad apples, but most of us are well-intentioned, basically we're good people". So we think. But look more deeply into every human soul. We're all addicted to someone or something other than God to quench our most profound human thirst, to matter, to be loved.

Sheer foolishness, for which we're each responsible. And yet we excuse ourselves. Our choices don't feel like choices. We have no control over them. We're addicted. We're victims of a pernicious disease, addiction. And that's exactly how it seems to us. We're no more responsible for our moral failure than I am for contracting cancer. It's not my fault. Help me. Treat me.

Apart from choices informed by truth from God and influenced by an intense thirst for God, everyone chooses wrongly. No one seeks for God, the only One who can free us from the control of self-centeredness, who will free us to love like Jesus. But why? Why does it require the Spirit of God to draw us to the free gift of life? Are we all that foolish?

I don't understand it, but Scripture teaches it. With Adam and Eve, somehow we've all grabbed fruit from the forbidden tree in Eden, the tree of the knowledge of good and evil, and not only eaten but digested it till it has corrupted the gift of freedom. The arrogance is beyond dispute. We have claimed the right to make choices informed by what seems true to us and influenced by whatever thirst in the moment most demands quenching. We're now imprisoned within the walls of self-centeredness, self-management, self-enhancement, and self-protection. We've declared our independence from God's ruling authority and benevolent wisdom. We've raised the flag of personal freedom.

The result? Addictions! A Primary Addiction to Self, and a host of Secondary Addictions to feeling good, on our terms and under our control. We've lost our freedom to choose glad surrender to God's love. Addiction has become a way of life so deeply ingrained in our being that only the Gospel can rescue us.

A brief comment off to the side. Given our mind-body connection, substances can become physically addicting to the degree that physical/chemical treatment may be required to enable the choice to resist the temptation to use the substance for relief from pain and a moment of consuming pleasure. But beneath the physical difficulties, the element of corrupt choice remains. Our predilection toward self-centeredness, our sin nature, is still the final culprit.

And yet, as mentioned before, even exhorting Christians equipped with a new, other-centered nature to choose well typically produces little more than shallow, temporary improvement. The compulsion to sin remains. By God's standard of holiness, only choices informed by God's truth and influenced by human thirst for God will be restored as free choices to resist addictive urges and to love sacrificially, like Jesus. *The freedom to choose the good nudges aside the compulsion to do bad.*

―

Now to the personal word. I'm writing this book as a fellow struggler, still drawn to relief and pleasure on my terms but now liberated by the Spirit to recognize my thirst for what only God provides and to seek after it. As completely as possible, I want to recover the power to choose wisely and well. To put it into one sentence, I want to know what it means for me, in the middle of my impatience with others and disappointment with myself, to know that Christ is in me as my firm hope for the full satisfaction of my deepest longings, tomorrow, when Jesus returns.

What I've just finished writing so far in this chapter came to mind with new clarity last night. Insomnia has its advantages, more private quiet time to think. I saw the Gospel as a north star guiding me across stormy seas of addiction toward the safe harbor of freely chosen self control.

For years, my wife has seen me live as a tortured soul, wanting to experience me as a settled man. I share the dream. Beneath the inevitable heartaches, uncertainties, and disappointments that come our way in this fallen world, I long to experience, to know, a solid peace, a settled hope that all things do work together for the good of Christ's disciples.

I tasted settledness last night. The taste is sweet. It developed in a storm of unsettledness that seemed more threatening than previous storms.

Something was happening. Familiar temptations receded into the shadows, still there but no longer on center stage. The value of waiting for the Second Coming; the sincere pursuit of spiritual formation; the appeal of sharing in the love the Son enjoys from His Father – everything I had written about in the first fourteen chapters seemed to come together. I *believed* Gospel truth. I *felt* my thirst for God. I knew I was free; I could choose to say no to the world, the flesh, and the devil. I could resist addictive urges. I was free to walk the narrow road to the life I most wanted. At least in that moment.

I was surrounded by wonderful mystery. It all just happened. Yet I wanted to know whatever I could know about the process of seeing hope restored, of recovering the freedom to walk past the forbidden tree and sit under the tree of life, nibbling on its fruit.

I've studied cognitive psychology; I was trained in behavioral psychology. I know something of cognitive behavior therapy that teaches a form of mindfulness, of replacing disruptive thoughts with productive thoughts. I understand the essence of family systems psychology. I've sat with families in my counseling office, helping each member recognize their role in generating distance and conflict.

But even during graduate school days, I was most drawn to depth psychology, an exploration into the dynamics roiling within people that may be responsible for so many of our problems. That approach seemed most consistent with Scripture. Scripture itself, we're told in Hebrews 4:12[3], functions like a sharp two-edged sword that discerns "the thoughts and intentions of the heart".

In the Psalms, David wanted to know what was going on in him that led him away from God. He asked God to search his heart, to explore him to know his thoughts (see Psalm 139:23)[4]. Sounds akin to dynamic therapy. As does Proverbs 20:5, "The purpose in a man's heart is like deep water"[5], difficult to identify, "but a man of understanding will draw it out."

With those passages in mind, I engaged myself in conversation last night, choosing to open myself to the Spirit's penetrating wisdom. It was then about four in the morning. Two words fastened themselves in my mind: LISTEN and UNDERSTAND.

I listened to my soul. Within minutes I could see myself as a young boy crying out to mother and dad, loving parents both, to relieve a terrible sense of aloneness. I felt terror, the terror of knowing that no one could fill the deepest void within me. I couldn't live with that fear.

I sensed what was going in me then, seventy years ago, and still going on now. I knew. I understood: *it was up to me.* I must do something to relieve the devastating pain of relational poverty, the aloneness that was tearing me apart, the sense of a void within me where fullness belonged.

From my earliest days, the stage was set. I would be funny, a successful student, a good person, a loyal friend – whatever I could do to get what I wanted from the people in my life. But I knew it would never be enough. So I buried my deep thirst beneath forced self confidence: I could pull it off. I could do enough to prevent myself from falling apart into a muddle of despair.

Residual fear that I couldn't pull it off became an angry demand that others do whatever they could to help me. But I didn't want to present myself as a weak, annoying leech, the proverbial tick looking for a dog.

At some point, nearing five o'clock this morning, I gave up. I was a mess of terrified, self-serving dynamics, motivations rooted in my flesh, not in God's Spirit. It was a relief to stand scared and helpless and alone before God. The welcome words of Jesus became almost audible: "Do not fear". Then I understood, not that I could pull it off, but that I couldn't. When God sees emptiness in someone's soul, His love requires Him to do something.

Truth swept through me like a cool breeze on a hot day: the atonement, forgiveness, God's calling on my life, His love for me as His son, the patience of the Spirit in forming me, the Second Coming, the hope of glory because Christ was in me.

In that moment I wanted nothing more than to know God and the power of His resurrection. The gift of choice seemed well informed by Gospel truth and strongly influenced by thirst. I sensed the power within me to say no to whatever put distance between me and my Father, between me and the Son, between me and the Spirit.

I rested. I was settled. I did not feel alone. I slept. At seven thirty this morning I woke up. I wanted to sing as I got myself ready to move into my day. I felt clearly moved to sing two songs, one an old Gospel chorus, the other an old Gospel hymn. The words to both found my voice:

The chorus:

> "Thank You Lord, for saving my soul.
> Thank You Lord, for making me whole.
> Thank You Lord, for giving to me

Your great salvation so rich and free".

The hymn: I sang all five verses several times. I'll mention just the first and last.

"Praise the Savior ye who know Him,
Who can tell how much we owe Him.
Gladly let us render to Him
All we have and are.

Then we shall be what we should be.
Then we shall be what we would be.
Things that are not now nor could be
Soon shall be our own."

Then the day got underway. A few bills to pay. Emails that needed a response. Phone calls to make. I was no longer flying high with passion. But I was settled. I knew I was in Christ, that He was my hope of glory.

I'll still stumble, and sometimes fail. The appeal of addictive urges will again assault me. When I do fail, I'll celebrate forgiveness. When I resist temptation, I'll celebrate the Spirit's work in me.

So now I wait, slowly learning to demand nothing now, not the pleasures of sin, not the response from others I still long for; and to expect everything when Jesus returns, no thirst left unquenched.

Still waiting. Now I better know what I'm waiting for, even when life gets frightening. My choices are better informed and more influenced by holy thirst.

It helped that I looked inside. Real change begins on the inside, then moves out – into freedom.

In moments of temptations, Christians need to remember what's true.

Sometimes truth seems far away.

It never is.

AFTERWORD

Why Wait For Heaven? I'm Living Here—Now!

No one will be interested in waiting for a heaven where white-robed holy people sit on clouds and strum harps forever. And at the other extreme, too few have gotten in touch with their thirst to relate to others with pure love. We're still more interested in being loved well by others.

Even fewer Christians have awakened to their deepest desire to literally see and enjoy Jesus. To many, the prospect seems more sweet than satisfying, too religious, not real.

It would be difficult, maybe impossible, for a child living among a tribe of impoverished people in Africa without access to water, school, doctors, or playgrounds to wait eagerly for a promised trip to Disney World, or even to McDonalds. Roller coasters and hamburgers? Beautifully dressed princesses and chocolate milk shakes? No image of happiness would form in the mind of the young girl.

"You can go to heaven some day."

"What's that? I want a better life now, a decent meal, someone to take care of me when I feel sick."

Why would anyone, whether in Africa, Iran, France, or America, wait for whatever might be our vision of heaven when we're thirsty for something else? It's more than sad, but the exquisite joy of being with Jesus in a perfect world fails to touch many Christians who are aware of stronger desires for less.

But suppose heaven satisfies every *lesser* legitimate thirst, for the end of injustice, for the end of greed, oppression, class warfare, unfair courts, rape; for the provision of meaningful work, perfect health, no reason to cry, new spheres of knowledge, and a kind of rest that makes no responsibilities tiresome.

Mozart died at thirty-five. Will his genius die with him? Or is he even now stunning new friends with recently written intricate melodies? Is my father sitting around, wondering what he could do to relieve boredom? Or are his intellectual abilities, so undeveloped through years of hard work to support the family, now reaching one crest after another. For everyone there, will mountains of desire be climbed with joy, realizing sheer delight, only to realize even deeper desires are yet to be satisfied?

Perhaps we need to awaken the thirst in that young African girl for always available pure water before we speak of the thrill of meeting Jesus. Maybe we should see into our souls to realize the legitimate pleasures of good marriages, good friends, good health, good jobs, and good ministries leave vague, buried, but real thirst unquenched.

I don't envision heaven as sitting at the feet of Jesus, always feeling a deepening delight in His presence. I do believe such delight will be the center of heaven. But that center will ripple out, perhaps into more and far better books coming from my pen, maybe truths so unworldly they will read like novels. I might attend an Elvis concert, even sing with him, while you wander through a museum of new paintings by Raphael, or listen to an opera singer you never heard of till you arrived in heaven.

I picture Billy Graham and a Christian social activist having a great time together "You brought fresh water to that African tribe, along with schools and electricity. You gave them hope that there is a God who cares. And then that young girl, now awake with thirst for more, watched me on television and realized her deepest thirst was to know Jesus as her Savior, her friend and her hope. So good working together".

And Jesus smiles.

—

His mother died. Her son missed his mother. But he gave way to spiritually alive imagination. He wrote a series of letters that he imagined his mother might write from heaven, letters addressed to her son and daughters, and signed "Mother".

In one, "mother" wrote something like this:

> "I can't tell you how wonderful it is here. Beyond anything I could have dreamed. I want to tell you what little I can put into words. Oh, wait a minute. There's a knock on my door. A man just told me I would have to go back into your world. I shouted 'No! No! It's too good here to go back even to all that was good there.' The man left. I just asked my friend who he was. She answered, 'Oh, that's Lazarus. He tells that to all the newbies here'. I laughed. I'm staying here! With more love than I ever was capable of, Mother"

That is true. The brother wrote those letters and sent them all to his sisters. The letter I just wrote is my memory of one that he wrote. His letter was far better.

My father's father died when my dad was 5 years old. When dad was in his early 80's, he told me that one night he was suddenly awakened from a sound sleep, strangely aware of two words, *sheer delight*. And then he became clearly aware of his father's presence, not visually, but somehow truly.

My father sat up, aware that the man he once called Papa was with him, and said, "Papa, what's it like up there?" Then inaudibly but as clearly as if the words reached his physical ears, he heard his Papa reply, "I don't want to ruin the surprise. It's better than I could ever describe. See you soon."

—

No description of heaven is adequate. The best we can do is to become aware of whatever thirst feels deeply alive in us, and then anticipate its complete satisfaction. Over time, anticipate becoming aware of actually meeting Jesus, face to face, and allow the "sheer delight" to move you toward WAITING FOR HEAVEN.

Acknowledgments

Most authors agree writing is a lonely business. For years I wrote in coffee shops, sitting by myself in an almost quiet corner, still hearing the chatter of others and the droning of background music that somehow increased a strangely welcome sense of isolation. I was chatting with no one and didn't bother to notice if I enjoyed the music or not. I was alone with my thoughts, aware of little else than where they were taking me. For the past 20 years, I've been writing either in a basement study in our Denver home or now in the loft of our current home in Charlotte.

But eliminate both mind-stirring conversations with others and soul-encouraging support from others and either I wouldn't write at all or I would produce even worse books than I've already authored. (Pardon a disingenuous nod to humility).

The team of Larger Story, a ministry envisioned and now wisely led by my older son Kep along with his most capable colleagues Kris and Karlene, has been with me and for me all the way. *Waiting for Heaven* is the first of hopefully quite a few more books published by Larger Story Press. The book would be far less without you, maybe non-existent.

And let me add a most grateful thank you to all who contributed funds to support the cost of publishing *Waiting for Heaven*. Your help in launching this book is much appreciated.

Conversations, either over breakfast or by phone with soul-mates Trip Moore, Jim Kallam, Mimi Dixon, and Steve Shores, have been keeping my old brain almost youthfully alive, enabling me to think as I write, often in deeply Christian categories supplied and sharpened by these friends.

And SSDers, you know who you are. But you have little idea of what you've meant to my spiritual life over these past 20 years.

Small groups can be over-rated. But when they're not, they are valuable beyond the ability of words to say. Tom and Jenny, Bob and Claudia, and my wife Rachael and I have been together for coming up on 2 decades. Open sharing with a genuine burden to be with each other on our spiritual journeys has made me gratefully aware that God's Spirit is still working in me, both as I relate and write.

Family, impossible to over-rate: Kep and Kimmie, Ken and Lesley, five grandchildren who love their grandparents, and an always interested and supportive sister-in-law Phoebe, widowed by my brother's death decades ago, surround me with prized opportunities to give and receive.

As I write, nearly 54 years of always deepening oneness with Rachael stirs a gratitude to God that sustains my longing to love her well and serve Him well.

Aloneness and community: the platform for living well.

P.S. If I were to name the many others whose friendship has encouraged me to keep thinking and writing, the list would become a long chapter in this book. Thank you to all!

Notes

Forward – Passages in Scripture to reflect on as you read this book:
1. *Holy Bible.* New International Version. Zondervan Publishing House, 1984. John 14:3.
2. *Holy Bible.* New Living Translation. Wheaton, Ill: Tyndale House Publishers, 2004. Hebrews 13:14
3. *Holy Bible.* The Message (MSG). Edited by Eugene H. Peterson, NavPress, 1993. Peter 2:11.

A Parable
1. *Holy Bible.* 1 Corinthians 15:19.

Prologue
1. *Holy Bible.* 2 Peter 1:3.

Introduction
1. Crabb, Lawrence J. *Inside Out.* NavPress, 1988.
2. *Holy Bible.* Galatians 1:6.
3. *Holy Bible.* 2 Peter 1:3.

Chapter One
1. Séneca Lucio Anneo, and James S. Romm. *How to Die: An Ancient Guide to the End of Life.* Princeton University Press, 2018.
2. *Holy Bible.* Gospel of Matthew.
3. *Holy Bible.* Gospel of Mark.
4. *Holy Bible.* Gospel of Luke.

5. Crabb, Larry J. *When Gods Ways Make No Sense.* Baker Pub., 2018.
6. *Holy Bible.* 1 Peter 1:13.
7. *Holy Bible.* Romans 8:23.
8. McKelvey, Douglas Kaine. *Every Moment Holy.* Nashville, TN, Rabbit Room Press, 2017.

Chapter Two

1. *Holy Bible.* Romans 7 verses 8 and 14.
2. *Holy Bible.* Romans 1:1.
3. *Holy Bible.* Romans 7: verses 15 and 19.
4. *Holy Bible.* Hebrews 11:25.

Chapter Three

1. C.S. Lewis quote
2. *Holy Bible.* 2 Corinthians 13:5.
3. *Holy Bible.* 1 Corinthians 3:13-15.
4. *Holy Bible.* 2 Corinthians 4:17.

Chapter Four

1. *Holy Bible.* New Living Translation. Wheaton, Ill: Tyndale House Publishers, 2004. Ephesians 1:7-9.
2. *Holy Bible.* New Living Translation. Wheaton, Ill: Tyndale House Publishers, 2004. Ephesians 1:10 and 14.
3. *Holy Bible.* New Living Translation. Wheaton, Ill: Tyndale House Publishers, 2004. 2 Corinthians 8:19.
4. *Holy Bible.* New Living Translation. Wheaton, Ill: Tyndale House Publishers, 2004. 1 Peter 5:10.
5. *Holy Bible.* New Living Translation. Wheaton, Ill: Tyndale House Publishers, 2004. Revelation 21:5.

6. *Holy Bible.* Kenneth Wuest Translation. Hebrews 10:24.
7. *Holy Bible.* Hebrews 11:26.
8. *Holy Bible.* New Living Translation. Wheaton, Ill: Tyndale House Publishers, 2004. Psalm 27:14.
9. *ESV: Study Bible.* English Standard Version. Wheaton, Ill: Crossway Bibles, 2007. Psalm 37:34.
10. *Holy Bible.* New Living Translation. Wheaton, Ill: Tyndale House Publishers, 2004. Matthew 28:19.
11. *Holy Bible.* New Living Translation. Wheaton, Ill: Tyndale House Publishers, 2004. Colossians 4:5.
12. *ESV: Study Bible.* English Standard Version. Wheaton, Ill: Crossway Bibles, 2007. Lamentations 3:26.
13. *Holy Bible.* New Living Translation. Wheaton, Ill: Tyndale House Publishers, 2004. Jeremiah 29:5.
14. *ESV: Study Bible.* English Standard Version. Wheaton, Ill: Crossway Bibles, 2007. Galatians 5:5.
15. *Holy Bible.* New Living Translation. Wheaton, Ill: Tyndale House Publishers, 2004. Philippians 1:6, Crabb's emphasis.
16. *ESV: Study Bible.* English Standard Version. Wheaton, Ill: Crossway Bibles, 2007. 1 Thessalonians 1:9.
17. *Holy Bible.* Hebrews 10:24.

Chapter Five

1. Ryle, John C. *Holiness.* Perfect Library, 1877.
2. *ESV: Study Bible.* English Standard Version. Wheaton, Ill: Crossway Bibles, 2007. Hebrews 11:24-26.
3. *Holy Bible.* Exodus 2:1-10.

Chapter Six

1. *Holy Bible.* Hebrews 11:24-26.
2. *Holy Bible.* New Living Translation. Wheaton, Ill: Tyndale House Publishers, 2004. Exodus 2:11.
3. *Holy Bible.* New Living Translation. Wheaton, Ill: Tyndale House Publishers, 2004. Exodus 2:13.
4. *Holy Bible.* New Living Translation. Wheaton, Ill: Tyndale House Publishers, 2004. Exodus 2:14.
5. *Holy Bible.* New Living Translation. Wheaton, Ill: Tyndale House Publishers, 2004. Numbers 11:10.
6. *Holy Bible.* New Living Translation. Wheaton, Ill: Tyndale House Publishers, 2004. Numbers 11:14.
7. *Holy Bible.* New Living Translation. Wheaton, Ill: Tyndale House Publishers, 2004. Hebrews 4:15.
8. *Holy Bible.* New Living Translation. Wheaton, Ill: Tyndale House Publishers, 2004. Philippians 1:29.
9. *Holy Bible.* New Living Translation. Wheaton, Ill: Tyndale House Publishers, 2004. 1 Peter 1:6.
10. *Holy Bible.* New Living Translation. Wheaton, Ill: Tyndale House Publishers, 2004. Numbers 20:3-5.
11. *Holy Bible.* New Living Translation. Wheaton, Ill: Tyndale House Publishers, 2004. Numbers 20:8.
12. *Holy Bible.* New Living Translation. Wheaton, Ill: Tyndale House Publishers, 2004. Numbers 20:10-11.
13. *Holy Bible.* Deuteronomy 33:1.

Chapter Seven

1. Francis Schaeffer comment

Chapter Nine

1. *Holy Bible.* 1 John 1:8.

Chapter Ten

1. Pope Benedict XVI quote

Chapter Eleven

1. *Holy Bible.* New Living Translation. Wheaton, Ill: Tyndale House Publishers, 2004. 1 Peter 1:13.
2. *Holy Bible.* New Living Translation. Wheaton, Ill: Tyndale House Publishers, 2004. Philippians 1:6.
3. *Holy Bible.* New Living Translation. Wheaton, Ill: Tyndale House Publishers, 2004. Ezekiel 36:27.
4. Brennan Manning quote
5. *Holy Bible.* New Living Translation. Wheaton, Ill: Tyndale House Publishers, 2004. 2 Timothy 4:3.
6. *Holy Bible.* Hebrews 10:24.

Chapter Twelve

1. *Holy Bible.* New Living Translation. Wheaton, Ill: Tyndale House Publishers, 2004. Titus 2:11-12.

Chapter Thirteen

1. *Holy Bible.* Colossians 1:22.
2. *Holy Bible.* John 15:12.
3. *Holy Bible.* Genesis 2:17.
4. *Holy Bible.* Joshua 29:15.
5. *Holy Bible.* Philippians 4:8.
6. *ESV: Study Bible.* English Standard Version. Wheaton, Ill: Crossway Bibles, 2007. 2 Timothy 3:14.

7. *Holy Bible.* John 8:32.
8. *ESV: Study Bible.* English Standard Version. Wheaton, Ill: Crossway Bibles, 2007. Philippians 2:13.
9. *ESV: Study Bible.* English Standard Version. Wheaton, Ill: Crossway Bibles, 2007. Romans 1:18-10.
10. *Holy Bible.* James 1:2-4.
11. *Holy Bible.* Hosea 7:14.
12. *ESV: Study Bible.* English Standard Version. Wheaton, Ill: Crossway Bibles, 2007. Psalm 73:28.
13. *ESV: Study Bible.* English Standard Version. Wheaton, Ill: Crossway Bibles, 2007. Psalm 42:1.

Chapter Fourteen

1. *ESV: Study Bible.* English Standard Version. Wheaton, Ill: Crossway Bibles, 2007. John 16:22.
2. *Holy Bible.* John 3:16.
3. *Holy Bible.* Roman Chapters 1-8.
4. Stott, John R. W. *The Cross of Christ.* IVP Books, 2006.

Chapter Fifteen

1. *ESV: Study Bible.* English Standard Version. Wheaton, Ill: Crossway Bibles, 2007. Romans 3:11-12.
2. *ESV: Study Bible.* English Standard Version. Wheaton, Ill: Crossway Bibles, 2007. Psalm 14:2.
3. *Holy Bible.* Hebrews 4:12.
4. *Holy Bible.* Psalm 139:23.
5. *Holy Bible.* Proverbs 20:5.

SPIRITUALLY HUNGRY?

JOIN THE ADVENTURE
LIVE THE LARGER STORY
LARGERSTORY.COM

Welcome to LARGER STORY

Here at LARGER **STORY**, we believe that God has called us to a beautiful adventure, enlarging our hearts to desire the Trinity above all else so that our lives may each tell the story of God by how we relate.

Based on the gospel-centered framework of Dr. Larry Crabb, LARGER **STORY** offers online resources and intentional pathways to spiritually hungry people who long to live fearlessly and are willing to ask the hard questions.

The Legacy of Dr. Larry Crabb

Through his storied 40-year publishing career, Dr. Larry Crabb has been sharing the movement of God in his own soul and through his story. In every book, article, sermon, or seminar, Larry reminds us to see the hand of God and hear His voice in any circumstance

and condition of our soul. We have amassed the prolific lifework of Larry Crabb here as a resource for anyone seeking to authentically and consistently live out the larger love story God is still telling every day. Our resource library includes:
- Videos
- Audios
- Books
- Webinars and Podcasts
- Blogs
- Spiritual Direction Resources

Join the Adventure

Find out what it means to live in the LARGER **STORY** *of God as we stumble through our smaller story with its everyday hassles, pleasures, trials, and blessings. When we tag along with what God is up to, we can find joy in the middle of heartache, hope in the middle of despair, faith in the middle of doubt – all through relating well in community. Join us on this grand and beautiful adventure!*

www.largerstory.com
hello@largerstory.com

Also by Larry Crabb

Inside Out
Finding God
Men and Women
The Adventures of Captain Al Scabbard: The Baron's Code
The Adventures of Captain Al Scabbard: An Unlikely Smuggler
Basic Principles of Biblical Counseling
Effective Biblical Counseling
God of My Father
Connecting
Understanding Who You Are
Marriage Builder
Encouragement
Fully Alive
Shattered Dreams
The Silence of Adam/ Men of Courage
Soul Talk
The Pressure's Off
Understanding People
PAPA Prayer
66 Love Letters
Hope When You're Hurting
Real Church
A Different Kind of Happiness
When God's Ways Make No Sense
How to Become One with Your Mate
Becoming True Spiritual Community
Who We Are & How We Relate